The Warriors' Code

The Warriors' Code

by
Dory J. Peters

BONNEVILLE BOOKS™

Springville, Utah

ISBN: 1-55517-613-5
v.1

Published by Bonneville Books
Imprint of Cedar Fort Inc.
www.cedarfort.com

Distributed by:

Typeset by Kristin Nelson
Cover design by Adam Ford
Cover design © 2002 by Lyle Mortimer

Printed in the United States of America
10 9 8 7 6 5 4 3 2 1

Printed on acid-free paper

Library of Congress Cataloging-in-Publication Data

Peters, Dory J.
  The warriors' code / by Dory J. Peters.
      p. cm.
  ISBN 1-55517-613-5 (pbk. : alk. paper)
  1. Mormons--Fiction. 2. Navajo Indians--Fiction. 3. World War,
1939-1945--Fiction. I. Title.
  PS3616.E84 W37 2002
  813'.6--dc21

                              2002000172

For the Navajo Code Talkers of World War II;
for their valor and courage,
and for the honor they brought
to the Diné (Navajo People), past and present.

And for the men and women
of the United States Armed Forces
who have fought and continue to fight
for the freedom of this great nation.

1

The sun was setting across the red Arizona valley. The evening brilliance made the towering red rock formations more spectacular than usual. The dry desert below was in direct contrast to the deep green of the ponderosa pine trees that surrounded the Chuska Mountain Range. This evening felt special as Lee rode back from a long day of cattle chasing. Finally the cattle were secure in the family homestead, not far from their home.

Lee's horse was just as tired as he was. Lee loved his companion that he had grown up with. He had named her *So'Doo Nidizidi* (Morning Star) because she was born in the morning and because of the white star on her nose; the rest of her was chocolate brown.

Lee and his twin brother had spent the better part of the last two days in the high Chuskas searching for lost cattle. They thought that rounding them up would have been an easy task, but it ended up being much more than they had bargained for.

The tall pine and ponderosa trees and lush green surroundings made it a more comfortable ride home, and home was where he wanted to be. It would be good to rest and have a solid meal.

As he rode he started to feel uneasy again. For the last few days he had felt as if he weren't riding alone, as if someone were watching him ride down the winding mountain trail.

Lee felt a cool evening breeze forming behind him. He pulled back on his horse's black mane. He quickly remembered the pain in his left arm and felt the warmth of fresh blood trickling down, and he placed his right hand over the wound to stop the bleeding again and. . . smiled to himself.

So'Doo Nidizidi suddenly stopped and nervously tamped her hoofs on the red dirt. Her startled movements told Lee something unfamiliar was near.

"Easy girl. I can feel it, too," he said, leaning forward to whisper into her ear. He slowly reached for his rifle, hoping not to bring too much attention.

His eyes slowly moved back and forth to first see what was out there before it saw them. But he had a feeling that whatever it was already knew they were there.

"Nothing," he said to himself.

The breeze seemed to pick up speed as it cleared the dense pinon forest and Lee's straight long black hair began to blow across his face as he turned to catch the full effect of the wind.

"What will it tell me today?" Lee murmured, turning to receive the wind.

He breathed deeply as the wind hit him.

Rain—in a day or so, he thought. "Good, we need the rain," he said aloud.

The cool air comforted him from the hot summer day and he felt renewed.

Moments later he again had the same feeling he was not alone. He looked around as if he might see someone, and prepared himself for a confrontation. And he nudged *So'Doo Nidizidi* toward home.

"There!" he said to himself.

In the lowest branch of a huge pine tree perched a white owl, watching, staring. The owl did not move, but he looked as if he were waiting for Lee to notice him.

Lee got off his horse slowly so he would not startle the owl. The owl tilted its head to one side then the other, as Lee moved. The owl was not afraid of him but seemed to want a closer look at Lee. They both stared at each other for a moment. There was a minute of complete silence that seemed like hours. Lee felt numb as if he were in a trance. He quickly felt uncomfortable and snapped out of it. He noticed himself still staring in the same place, though the owl had now disappeared.

His father had taught Lee that seeing an owl during the day meant that there was a message or even death was coming in the near future.

I wonder what is going to happen? He thought, curious and intrigued by what it meant. *I hope it's good luck,* he thought.

"And I'm not afraid of death!" he said aloud.

This was the only the second time in his life that he had seen a regular owl during the day but not a white one. Eager to tell his father about what he had seen, he tried to hurry himself a little more.

There's the ridge before I reach home, he thought. *I can smell fresh cedar burning. That means that mother is preparing something good and the dogs are starting to bark at my return.*

"Home!" he said.

Lee surveyed his home nestled in a large grassy knoll surrounded by hundred-year old ponderosa pine trees. The tall green giants seemed to reach up and touch the sky. There was a small creek nearby that horses often drank from and that the family used to irrigate their small farm. The land was lush and green with areas of scrub oak. And the sand that covered the landscape was a beautiful deep red. The sheep corral near the hogan was made of wood kept neat and clear of any imperfection. It held up to a hundred sheep, and the horses were kept in a fairly large corral only for their protection from mountain lions and wolves. Almost in the center of the area, sat a small hogan, a mud and wood home that his father and grandfather had built years ago. The entrance faced east. Navajo culture dictated that an entrance of a home must face east so that one can meet and greet the morning sun. This ensured that he or she would be in harmony each day. All of the surrounding dwellings were built in the Navajo tradition. Off to the distance next to the creek was a small mud sweat lodge for cleansing oneself from evil or sickness and performing other ceremonies that took place there.

He could see the smoke rising from the center of the home. It was getting dark. He looked back to see if he could see his brother. The sun was now setting behind the mountain where he knew his brother was. He was hoping that his brother was okay, but knew that if something was wrong, he would know. All their life they had been able to sense each other's feelings, even when they were apart. He turned back.

So'Doo Nidizidi started into a full gallop and Lee stopped trying to hold him back. They were both eager to eat and rest. Lee's year-old sheep dog ran up to greet him, his tongue hanging out between the barks. His joyful dancing back and forth made Lee grin and he jumped off *So'Doo Nidizidi* to say hello before his dog wore himself out.

"Well, hello *Ch'iizhi*. It seems you have missed me," Lee said, kneeling down and scratching the top of his furry head. *Ch'iizhi* placed his front two paws on Lee's shoulders and began licking his face, his tail wagging violently.

"Okay, okay, good to see you," Lee laughed and stood up.

Ch'iizhi started to bark again telling everyone of Lee's arrival, and the rest of the dogs chimed in.

This is a really beautiful place to live, but why do I feel that I'm not going to be here very long? He looked down into the desert where the table mesas and Shiprock wall are. Just beyond the desert he stared at what was once his ancestor's homeland about hundred miles away—Mesa Verde, Colorado.

He turned back around to enter the hogan.

He stopped and looked back over the valley again.

The cool evening was beginning and the moon was already up and full and the stars were coming out. The sounds of another summer night were all around—crickets in the brush and off in the distance, a wolf was howling.

Ch'iizhi ran back and forth until they reached the hogan where the aroma of frybread and mutton was almost unbearable.

"I'm not going anywhere," he murmured.

Lee pulled back the thick woven rug covering the entrance of the home and stepped in.

"You're finally home," Mother said. She quickly noticed the blood on his sleeve and moved closer to inspect the wound. She looked up at Lee with a smile. "Are you two fighting again?"

Lee said nothing. His mind was elsewhere, trying to figure out why he was feeling that he would miss this place.

She ignored the fact that he didn't respond, which was typical of a Navajo male, and quietly replaced the soaked wrap with a fresh cloth. Then she continued to prepare the dinner.

Lee looked around his home as if he were entering it for the first time. The smell of home. There was the old small black wood burning stove in the center of the hogan. He loved to hear wood crackle while it burned, and he enjoyed seeing the different colors—the yellow, red and sometimes blue orange of the fire as he stared at it while father told stories during the evening. The two small beds nestled against the mud-covered wall of the hogan where his parents slept. He looked over to where he and his brother slept. He remembered when mother had first weaved their blankets from the sheep that they cared for. He remembered he and his brother gathering the plants and herbs with their mother during the summer and the stories that she shared when she first met their father and what the

5

different colors meant. She would always make a point to explain what each color meant as she was making their blanket.

The design for each blanket was a dream and she would sing a song as she made the blankets. Although the *Yebacheii* was the pattern for the region, Mother had made a special blanket for each boy from that dream. She had dreamed the pattern for Lee's blanket; it was the eagle and the wolf. The dream for Charlie's was the bear and deer. Lee remembered how he and Charlie would sit there in the corner next to father's bed during the winter while she told about her dreams and they would listen to her beautiful songs. She would tell them that they were young men and were not to participate in the singing, but because there were no females beside her it was okay. It seemed like that happened just yesterday.

He noticed his father was a strong man—a man that knew everything and was afraid of nothing. He wasn't even afraid of wild animals like the bears and mountain lions. Lee remembered their first hunt and how his father seemed so proud when Lee killed his first deer. Charlie hadn't been able to get a deer that season, but around that same time he did kill a mountain lion that had attacked the sheep.

Lee loved the stories of his ancestors, especially the stories of the great warriors. He and Charlie would always talk about becoming great medicine men like their father.

Lee smiled to himself as he watched his father stacking freshly cut wood.

"I know why you call that worthless dog *Ch'iizhi*," James said, pointing to the dismantled stack of kindling wood. "I just don't know why he chews on the firewood only when you are gone. I guess he has nothing better to do."

"James, it's not that bad. He's a good dog. He just seems to have a craving for wood," Mother answered.

Lee walked over to his father to help him. He got closer to get his attention.

"I saw a white owl at Sitting Wolf Rock today. I felt like it was watching me," Lee said, ignoring his father's previous comments.

James, undeterred from his task, asked, "Where's your brother? Is he coming?"

Lee was surprised by his father's attitude.

Something is bothering him. I see that pain in his eyes. It seems that he has been praying... I know that smell... I smell burnt sage or something. He has performed a ceremony...but for what? I wonder what's wrong?

"He said that he was coming right behind me," Lee answered. "He met Jimmy Yazzie at Wheatfield Lake. He just got back from the war and . . ."

James slowly rose and the wood dropped to the dirt floor with a hollow crash. He walked slowly to the door and stopped. His head was bowed and his back was toward Lee.

"I don't understand why we're fighting a war that we don't belong in," James said. He turned to face his son. "It's their war, not ours."

2

The piercing thunder crackled and rumbled between the Swiss Alps and into the tiny village of Grindelwald. In the top floor of the Hotel Steinbock, just off the Hauptstrausse, Victor immediately fell back into reality.

"Its only a dream . . . it's not real," he whispered to himself.

The sound echoed outside his window. He noticed that he had been sweating and was still unsure of where he was. He turned over, relieved to find that he was still with Allison, but surprised that she had not been awakened by the storm.

Scheisse, I am halfway around the world from Red Valley and I still can't escape this dream. It's the third time this week. It's almost as if I were there and each time I feel it becoming more intense. I don't need this right now. That part of my life is over. I have no reason to dream stuff like that. I don't have any desire go back there to live. Mom is okay. She likes it there but this is where I want to be, he thought as he reached for the bottle of Coke on his nightstand.

Feeling a sense of being suffocated as if the walls were closing in on him he quickly stumbled across the room toward the window and opened it. A flash of lightning illuminated the Valley as if it were midday; seconds later, heart-pounding thunder shook him to the core. Victor quickly shut the window and turned to return to bed, but the room had become dark again and, unable to judge the distance, he landed on Allison's leg.

Allison sat up and slapped Victor on the back. "Ouch! That hurt," she cried. "What are you doing?"

A little embarrassed, he asked, "Didn't you hear the storm outside?"

Allison was trying to focus her eyes to see the clock on the night stand. "It's 3:30 in the morning! What storm? I was asleep!" she growled as she wiped her eyes.

She turned on the bedroom lamp to get a better look at what was going on. She now realized rain was pounding down hard on the roof. lightning flashed, and seconds later came a huge sound of thunder. The windows shook again and she moved in closer to Victor.

As Victor turned to sit on the edge of the bed, Allison sensed something had happened. She turned his shoulders toward her and looked into his deep brown eyes.

"Vic, are you okay, honey?" she asked. "You look like you've seen a ghost or something."

"No, no, I'm okay. I just had a dream about my grandfather again. But this time it seemed more real."

"Do you want to talk about it?"

He didn't answer right away; but waited a few seconds.

"No . . . It's okay; you go back to sleep. I'm going to watch a little TV."

Allison, grateful to return to bed, quickly jumped under the comfortable thick fedder decker and fell back to sleep. Victor stared at the clock and tried to return to sleep but couldn't. The only sound he heard was the storm outside which was now slowly fading away. The only interesting program on TV was a rerun of "Frasier."

It's not the same in German, he thought.

The hours drifted by and Victor watched each minute pass.

At 7:30 a.m., feeling weary and miserable, he sat up again. The television was still on and Victor glanced over at the program that was now playing.

Hey, that looks like Regis and whoever that woman is. I

can't ever remember her name. It's still not the same in German.

He clicked off the TV, put his feet on the cold wooden floor and slowly stumbled to open the window. He stared out the window of his room. As always, he was still overwhelmed by the beauty of the mountain scenery. The morning mist was just beginning to break up. Victor looked up to the Alps and noticed the clear blue skies. He followed mountain peaks down to the water that fell freely from the middle of the shear rock faces and followed it until it disappeared into the morning mist.

He watched the steel blue water of the lake, its rivers scattered throughout the valley. The water looked as if it were ice cold. The chalet homes that dotted the base of the mountain were nestled neatly between more shades of green than could be seen anywhere on earth. Grindelwald was waking up.

Victor looked down on Main Street as the shops and businesses were beginning to open. The buildings were lined up next to each other just like a typical European Christmas snow village you could buy in America.

There is my competitor: Schweizerischer Bankverein. And right next to them is a new shop—it looks like a travel agency (Reiseburo Eiger). It looks like Herr Strupler owns the office. Of course Frau Meier, at the small backeri across the street is just opening her doors for business.

The smell of her fresh pastries filled the brisk morning sky. Victor took a deep breath of the fresh air. And as he stood looking out at the land of his second home, he wondered what it would have been like if he had never been able to experience this place.

I would have never met Frau Meier. She never wanted to talk to me about religion, but she would always want to talk about her first and only trip to America.

She said when she was a little girl she always wanted to visit

Arizona. This was very special to her because her father was a German soldier in World War Two. Her father had helped capture a couple of American soldiers who were later released after the war. During their detainment, her father befriended one of the American soldiers and later found out he was from Arizona and that he was an American Indian. She always got excited when she showed Victor the gift of an arrowhead that this soldier had given her father. She had studied English for two years before she went to Arizona to see if she could find this person or his family. She would always say, "You all look the same."

Victor laughingly told her, "I feel the same way about you white people." Unfortunately, she never found this person or his family but she loved to talk about it. Of course every time Victor visited, it would be the same story over and over again as if it had never been heard before. Victor always enjoyed her company even though she never joined the church.

It's going to be good to see her again, he thought as he looked down at her backeri.

Victor's mind quickly turned back to his recurring dream. As a boy he had tried so hard to forget about his nightmares. He would see himself in a strange land he had never visited before. He would be running from a hot fire and choking smoke that would eventually overtake him and he would feel the pains of death. Victor's Grandpa performed a ceremony for him, and sang a song that he needed to remember in case the dream came again.

But I can't remember it, he thought. *Well, it's been a long time. I'm not a kid anymore. I can handle this. The same way I always solve my problems—hit it head on and deal with it. Grandpa always said, "Get busy living or get busy dying." I don't know why I remember that but it seemed to work for me. But why do I feel that something is going to happen? I can't stop feeling that.*

3

"Vic, is something bothering you?" Allison asked as she got up from the bed and rummaged through the drawer for her clothes.

Victor turned to face her and smiled.

"What did you say, Hon?" Victor stepped closer to grab Allison. Hoping to change the subject, he hugged her from behind.

Allison, a little startled, said, "Hey, watch it! I'm trying to get ready." She pulled away, picked up her robe and towel and headed for the shower.

"Last night when you were talking about your grandpa I got thinking about the Rez. I hope that the boys are okay. I really miss them. It's been almost two weeks now." She sighed and climbed into the shower.

"Yeah, I know. I really miss them, too." Victor headed for the phone by the bed and stopped. "It's midnight in Red Valley," he said with disappointment and sat down. He rolled back into bed and closed his eyes as if he could sleep again.

A moment later Allison was drying her long brown hair with a towel and walked out of the steam-filled bathroom. She smiled at Victor on the bed. *He can go back to sleep faster than anyone I know.* She jumped on the bed next to him and slapped him on the behind.

"Hey, I'm trying to go back to sleep!" Victor slurred.

"The Hendersons are going to be here in a half-hour so you need to get up." Allison said as she jumped off the bed to find her clothes.

"Okay, I'll just lie here for a minute. I promise I'll get up. Just give me two more minutes." Victor got himself comfortable and started to close his eyes. He was startled by a glimpse of a white owl perched on the balcony. Victor jumped up quickly and ran to the window as the owl flew off. He looked to see where it went, but he couldn't see any sign of it. He felt a cold chill through his body and the hair on his back of his neck stood on end. Quickly shaking his head, he hurried for the bathroom, passing Ally sitting on the edge of the bed putting on her shoes.

Should I tell her or not? I don't want to freak her out. She has heard too many Skin Walker stories. I better not or she's not going enjoy the rest of our trip. Okay, I won't say anything, he thought as he walked into the humid bathroom.

Knock, knock, knock . . .

"Vic, they're here!" Allison yelled, surprised by the Hendersons' promptness. *They are ten minutes early!* Allison answered the door.

"*Gruezi wohl,* Allison," Ruth said with a smile. She hugged Allison and kissed her on each cheek.

"Oh huh, gruezi. Good morning, guys." Allison said, as she invited the Hendersons in.

"Hey, this is a pretty cool place," Don said, walking over to the window. "The view from here is incredible." He turned around just as Ruth started to knock on the bathroom door.

"Hurry up, I'm hungry. Are you going to be long?"

"Hey Ruth, let's eat at McDonald's today," Victor yelled from inside the shower.

"Ugh, Victor! You travel to Europe and all you can think about is eating American food. I'm sure we won't be able find one close enough," Ruth said, wincing.

"Come on, the nearest McDonald's is only twenty kilometers away," Victor replied. He knew that to get Ruth going, all you had to do was mention any of his favorite things like

McDonald's, Coke, or Twinkies.

Allison, embarrassed, shrugged her shoulders and said, "He has habit of knowing where all the McDonald's are. I think he just likes to give you a bad time."

"I know that, but the day is just getting started," she smiled.

Allison hurried through the suitcase to find something for Vic to wear and headed toward the bathroom and opened the door just enough to slip Victor's clothes through.

The shower stopped and Victor asked, "Are we still heading to Schilthorn and Lauterbrunnen today? I love those places. And we have to have dinner tonight at this place I know."

"Oh, you mean The Post? How do you expect us to forget that? It's all you have been talking about," murmured Ruth.

Victor opened the bathroom door to say hello. Everyone looked at him as if to say, "Yes, we are waiting," and he grinned and grabbed his shoes at the end of the bed.

"Okay guys, I'm ready and hungry I think we should pay Frau Meyer a visit," he announced as he tied up his shoes.

Victor stood up and grabbed their jackets and keys and they make their way out the door.

They walk quickly cross the cobblestone Hauptstrasse to the Backerei.

Frau Meier lit up with a smile as Victor's party entered the small bakery and she quickly walked from behind her counter to grab both his hands and pull him down to kiss his cheeks.

"I wondered if you were back in town. You haven't been by for a while," she said and she squeezed Allison's hand. Frau Meier was short and plump—a very typical aging Swiss woman. She reminded Victor of the German bar maids at the Octoberfest. She had always like Victor. The two had met while he was living in the area on his church mission and before Victor had even met her, he had been warned by his companion that she was not very friendly, but the moment she found out that he was American Indian the rest was history. Frau Meier felt she had known Victor his whole life and she even spoke to him as if they were old friends. Victor found that on more than one occasion during his mission he was faced with very similar experiences. People who would not even give Victor's white companions the time of day, would want to talk to Victor and would want to know about him. He felt almost like a celebrity.

Frau Meier quickly got behind the glass counter.

"I made this apple struddle the way you like it, with lots of apple! And look! Over there is a Coke machine. Also, I have ice you know, for the Americans. It's been real good for business," she laughed handing over the pastries.

They all chose something. He handed Frau Meier money to pay for the food. She took the money from his hand and placed it in her till. She then placed a Saint Gallen loaf of bread in a bag and handed it over the counter to Victor.

"You will need this for lunch," she said with a smile.

"It's your favorite, Ja?" she replied.

"It's gratis!"

"You can't do this every time I visit. You don't have to feed me. I can afford to buy my food now," he said.

Frau Meier took his hand and patted the back of it softly, and said with a smile, "You know I will always take care of my favorite Indian."

Victor leaned over the counter and kissed her cheek and they all waved *Aufwiedersehen* as they left the small store.

"Tomorrow, I'll be back to visit," Victor said as he left the store.

"I see you then," she said in her broken English, waving good-bye.

They walked back to the car and headed down the valley toward Lauterbrunnen.

It was nice to ride in a black fancy Mercedes 600 SEL and

smell the new pearl white leather with glossy wood panels. *It is every bit what the carmaker claimed it to be,* Victor thought. It was much different in contrast to the blue 1972 blue station wagon that his mother had in the mid-1980s. Then the seats were torn in places and were held together with duct tape or just covered with a blanket. There was an old, used eight-track tape deck that was purchased at a local flea market in Shiprock by his older sister. She had tried to install it herself to help improve the sound in the car but it rarely worked. When it decided to work you had your choice of, *The Best of Weylon Jennings* or *Boston,* both of which were typically found underneath the torn seats. Before the tape could be inserted into the tape deck, it would need a quick clean up. It usually contained at least one piece of chewed gum and sticky brown drops of Coke. The speakers of course, were filled with old potato chips, sand, and sticky cola so it was impossible to hear the sound. The car windows were usually down, but not by choice. Sometimes Victor tried to look through the garbage bags that had been taped into place with thick strips of duct tape. When it got colder the window would be covered completely with cardboard.

"It is nice to have the windows work," he mistakenly said aloud looking through the nicely tinted window has he watched the beautiful green hills go by.

"What?"

"What's wrong with the windows?" Don asked concerned, turning his head back to face Victor.

"Oh, nothing," Victor replied.

"Watch the road or the windows won't be working at all after we plummet off the cliff to our deaths," yelled Ruth.

Ignoring the conversation, Victor thought, *It's just so nice that we don't have to wear extra clothing and we don't have to yell to be heard, to enjoy a simple ride.*

Victor, exhausted and suffering sleep deprivation, began to fall asleep.

* * *

"Sonny, I can't hear you—come here closer. I'm sorry but the wind is too loud. I can't roll up the window. It's broken again," Betty yelled.

By the loud sound one would think that they were in the middle of a Nascar race. But traveling under fifty-five miles an hour it was hard to imagine. The poor car somehow continued to live. "This one should have been euthanized years ago," a mechanic in Shiprock had once said. "Put it down and leave it to the car gods." But it still defied the best auto mechanic's opinion.

And Betty would always say, "But we're still on the road."

Grandpa gave the car a blessing again, which explained the burnt smell of plants that lingered inside the car. Sheryl would complain that the smell would make her pee her pants, but Betty would always know that was only an excuse.

"Mom, it's really hot and I'm hungry, too," Victor complained.

The drive from Sheep Spring to Gallup was long and hot, and the old blue wagon was shaking from the tires all the way to the knobs on the radio. The dry summer heat was almost unbearable and the landscape was filled with rolling sand hills and tumbleweeds. The only enjoyment would be to hear Grandpa sing and tell stories. That is if you could hear him.

It was the first of the month. Betty, the family and Grandpa were on their way to Gallup to cash Grandpa's social security check and hopefully enjoy the monthly stop at Earl's Restaurant.

"Victor, this heat is nothing. When I was younger I used to run and work in this kind of heat. It was even hotter," Lee smiled.

"Grandpa, why did you like to work in the hot sun? I like it in the mountains better," Sheryl, Victor's little sister replied.

After cashing the check, they all headed to Earl's. Everyone was excited. Something about eating in the big city made it special to see all the cars and buildings. And sometimes they would get lucky and see a train go by—a favorite sight for Victor and his sisters. As they arrived, they entered the crowded restaurant. It always seemed busy, watching everyone going back and forth. Victor could hear only the voices of the people talking all at the same time. To him it sounded like running water. Everybody was in a hurry—unlike home where the only excitement was watching ants build an anthill. There was always a long wait as the white families behind them would be seated first, but no one objected to the treatment. They were used to it, so they waited.

They were finally seated to have lunch. They had a table adjacent to a white family with children that looked to be almost the same age as Betty's family. Sheryl noticed the young white girl that would have been about her same age. The young girl had bright blue eyes and her blonde hair was put up in pretty pink barrets. Her white shirt, denim overalls and clean white shoes looked new. The girl noticed Sheryl and smiled and gave her a small wave of hello. Sheryl took notice of her own clothes, her dirty red pants and torn red shirt. Her hands were dirty and her hair was windswept and unkempt. Sheryl responded with a wave in spite of her own outward appearance.

The mother of the white girl noticed the activity and quickly pulled the girl out of sight from Sheryl and whispered in her ear. She sat on the seat hidden from view. Betty also noticed the girl and quickly pulled Sheryl in and told her, "Sheryl, don't look at them or talk to them. You might get us in trouble. Just leave them alone. Maybe they won't kick us out. We just got here." She nervously pulled her in and told everyone not to look in their direction anymore.

19

Grandpa objected and said loudly in Navajo, "I'm tired of being treated this way—always having to feel that we have to wait at the back of the line so that white people can go first. We can't look at them like they're somebody special. They say that this is a free country but for who? I had friends that died for this country that were Navajo and I'm not afraid of them," Lee explained with authority.

But Betty, more worried now about being noticed, pleaded with her father not to make a scene as almost every one the restaurant was quiet. A man came over from behind the counter, wiping his hands. He was wearing a white apron and a white hat. He walked up to the table.

"Lady, if you're going to be loud you need to take your kind out of here. Especially your drunk husband, father or what ever he is. Understand?"

Betty quickly grabbed Lee's arm to keep him down. Lee's first instinct was to lay his fist across the man's face. But he looked at his grandchildren's faces, staring into their big brown eyes filled with fear, confusion and hunger. He was sure they were just hungry. He decided that this was not the time. He put his head down and said nothing.

"I'm sorry, mister. We'll be okay," Betty pleaded.

The white man just stared at them in disgust before he walked away and returned to his place behind the counter.

* * *

"Vic sweetie! Wake up! We're here," Allison said as she nudged him awake.

Forty-five minutes had gone by and they entered the small village of Stechelberg, nestled in a majestic green valley which had been carved by millions of years of glacier movement.

They finally found a parking place and they walked across the parking lot to the ticket office to purchase the tickets for the gondola ride to the top of Schilthorn.

This was the first time Allison had seen the area. She was amazed at the chalets that were so isolated in this part of the valley. The quiet on the mountain was interrupted only by the sounds of cowbells. The valley was covered with summer flowers of all colors—yellow, blue, purple and red. The water-falls were amazing to see as they fell freely from hundreds of feet above. The sun was not hidden by a single white cloud.

This is going to be a gorgeous day, Allison thought.

Victor and the Hendersons had a special relationship. For almost twelve years they had known each other. Ruth was the first to befriend Victor and from that day on their friendship had grown to more of a feeling of family than just friends. Years ago her daughter was very interested in American Indians. The elementary school announced that their next course of study would be of American Indians. This was the first time Katherine had any interest in school. Ruth, excited by her renewed interest in class, decided to help out trying to find anything or anyone that had Southwestern art or knew anyone that traveled to the Southwest. The ultimate bonus would be to have a real Indian. Through her personal prayers to help her daughter, Ruth, in her own words, said she was instructed to call the Mormon Missionary Home in Zurich. She called the Mormon Mission President and had asked if there were anyone in the mission who may be of American Indian descent or someone who knew an American Indian. The President told her that there was a full-blooded Navajo missionary that arrived the day before. In disbelief and excitement, she asked permission to contact Victor. The rest is history.

They entered the gondola and viewed the awe-inspiring mountain below. Victor asked, "Are there any owls around these areas, Don?"

"I'm not sure. I think we have them here, but I haven't personally seen any. Why do you ask?"

"Just wondering," Victor answered, hoping not to draw too much attention to himself, but still in a deep meditation over the white owl on his balcony.

Ruth was surprised by Victor's question. "I don't know why you are suddenly interested in wildlife," she said. "You are the only Indian I know that knows so much about investment banking and so little about nature."

"That's right, and I am the only Indian you know," Victor retorted.

Allison, meanwhile, focused her attention on her surroundings. Victor had often spoken about the beauty of this country, but she continued to be astounded at the new places she visited.

Everyone was immersed in their own quiet reflections when Victor noticed a bird high in the sky. It seemed to float on the air, soaring this way and that until it came close enough to recognize. Victor could tell it was a white owl and he could tell the owl knew where he was going, right toward Victor.

He wanted to let everyone be apprised of what he had earlier experienced but he felt almost a reverent respect for the messenger and kept the sight to himself.

What do you want? Is there something that I should know? I wish I knew what this all means, he thought to himself. *Grandpa could tell me all about you. I know that you are trying to tell me something. . . but what?*

As the gondola ascended the mountain, Allison's face stayed glued to the window, taking in all the beauty around her. And as the gondola stopped at the top, she felt as if she had just been placed in the middle of a bowl of whipped cream. Every peak was so white and wind-swept that the snow-capped mountains looked airy and soft, not icy and cold. Schilthorn restaurant was in front of them and they had climbed almost 3000 meters high. The restaurant, atop the mountain, slowly revolved so you could view the entire area without leaving your table. It was surprising that the popular restaurant was relatively slow. The normally crowded atmosphere was quiet and they found a table next to the window.

"When are you guys going home?" Don asked, wanting to make conversation.

"What Don is asking is whether Credit Suisse is going to relocate you here for good," Ruth added.

Victor was not surprised by Ruth's straight-forward question. "Well, I don't know," he replied. "The company has talked about relocating me here for a couple of years but we still don't know yet." He set his typical European large-small Coke down. "I ordered a large Coke. For three bucks, I can get three or four fountain drinks at the Thriftway in Shiprock." Victor laughed. Then he attempted to get back on track, "All my life I have worked to get to this point in my career. I have dreamt of living in Switzerland and spending time here and raising my family here. Just the other day, I met with Herr Brezne. You know him, don't you, Don?"

"Yeah, isn't he the guy that we went to dinner with the last time you were here?" Ruth recalled. "I wondered if he had a medical condition the way he was snorting and coughing at the dinner table. He reminded me of a cat I once had that had a hairball. He was so disgusting."

"It wasn't that bad," Don said.

"I guess once or twice isn't that bad, but every time anyone wanted to say something, he would say, 'excuse me.' And hack again." Ruth could see that she had gotten off the conversation somewhere and she stopped. "I'm sorry Victor, what were you saying?"

"If you guys are finished..." Victor smiled. They all grew quiet. "He offered me a permanent position here."

"That's *wunderbar*! Oh, I'm so excited for you!" Ruth

replied, but she noticed a look that she rarely saw in Victor's questioning stare. "Or not?" she added with a somber tone.

"No, no, don't get me wrong. Allison and I agree that this is a fantastic opportunity and I know it would be a great move, but there is just a feeling in the pit of my stomach that makes me question . . ."

Ruth knew the timing was wrong but still she said, "It was probably all of those pastries and junk food you consume daily."

Allison chuckled.

Don was surprised that after thirty years of marriage, Ruth could still catch him off guard.

Victor thought. *Maybe this isn't the time to talk about this. After all, we are on somewhat of a vacation and I don't need to bring everyone into my reality.*

"Touche, Ruth. I bet it is indigestion."

"So you're considering the offer?" Ruth excitedly asked.

"That will be great to have you close!" Don added.

I hope so, Victor thought.

4

A week later, Victor was back on the Navajo reservation. It was hard to get used to the dry heat. But this was home—where Victor had grown up. His ancestry and hundreds of years of history were here. It was hard to consider leaving, he thought, looking around his old stomping ground.

"Check this out, Vic. Do you remember this?" Raymond asked, holding a short stick that appeared to have been chewed on. He had removed it from the glove box of the old 1958 Chevy truck.

"Grandpa told us this story a hundred times, huh, Vic? That old crazy dog of his liked to chew on Great Grandpa's wood stuff and it drove him nuts. I don't know why he kept this old piece of wood in the truck. I guess he always wanted to remember his favorite pet."

The truck was half faded blue and half rust. Three of the four tires were flat and only one rim still had a hubcap. The oxidized hood of the beat-up truck was open and the front end was raised up on cinder blocks and planks of two-by-four wood.

Raymond Nakai, Victor's first cousin, had established himself as the czar of Grandpa's old truck.

The dry Arizona sun that seemed always hotter there than anywhere else was beating down on the pair.

The seventy-year-old Navajo Willow that Grandma planted when she was a teenager provided enough shade to cover the entire site.

The tree stood between the old hogan on the west, and

Grandma's newer house, which sat to the east. It was sad to see the farm in such disarray. There had seemed to be so much more prosperity around the area when Victor was younger. Grandpa and Uncle Roy and his other relatives had worked hard to care for the five hundred acres of surrounding fields which grandpa had acquired over the years of hard work.

As Victor looked around at the farm he wondered, *What if I had stayed? Would I have been in charge of this place? Was it wrong for me to go off and be a part of the white man's world? All of my decisions came at a cost. I am living the life I have always wanted. I didn't know. I have gained so much but I have so little. Have I contributed anything to my own people, or have I taken too much? Raymond's life is so simple, but he is always talking about how wonderful it used to be.*

Victor stood still as his eyes fell on the old swing hanging in the tree, it's wooden plank broken in two and dangling from the frayed rope.

I remember that day when Grandpa made that swing for us. . .

* * *

"Victor, look at what Grandpa made," Raymond yelled.

Victor's sister Pamela was sitting on the swing kicking her legs back and forth.

"Kids, you'd better enjoy your new swing before it gets too cold. Winter is just a few weeks away," Grandpa said with a smile.

Pamela screamed, "Raymond, I'm not getting off the swing yet! It's still my turn!"

The sun was setting on the fall evening, and before anyone noticed, it was dark. All the kids had taken their turn, and they sat contented under the tree and looked up at the falling stars.

Everything was quiet. They all lay down next to each other like sardines. It didn't matter where they laid—in the grass, or in the dirt—as long as they were comfortable.

"Hey Vic, What do you want to be when you grow up?" Ray asked, breaking the silence.

"I don't know Raymond. I don't think about it."

Raymond responded, "I want to be a white man like those guys in the big cities like Farmington; they live in those big houses and drive those nice cars. I want to be smart like them."

"I want to be a doctor so that I can fix people," Pamela mused.

Victor thought a moment and then said, "I know what I want to be now. I want to be like Grandpa, a medicine man."

* * *

"Hey Vic! Aren't you listening?" Raymond's voice broke the daydream.

Victor, startled from his memories, saw that Raymond had scooted under the truck on his back and had started tinkering and mumbling. The metal ratchets and screwdrivers made a hollow clang on the old engine. Victor grabbed a wooden chair and opened the small greasy cooler next to him. The cooler contained beer and a couple of cans of Coke. Victor closed the lid and leaned back looking at the job that Ray had ahead of him, knowing he wouldn't be of much help.

"Hey bro, how long you on the Rez?" Ray asked between grunts.

"What?" Vic answered, figuring he couldn't ignore Ray's chatter forever.

Ray was under the truck grunting and talking, so Vic crouched down to hear Ray a little better.

"What did you say, Ray?"

Ray's grease-covered blue coveralls started to move from under the truck, and he rolled from his back to his side and pursed his lips and pointed them in the direction of the rusty toolbox near the front of the truck. "Hand me the crescent wrench."

Victor twisted on the balls of his feet to turn toward the toolbox and grabbed the wrench. Turning back, he handed the wrench to Ray and snidely remarked, "Okay Shirley, here you go."

"What did you say?" Ray asked, surprised. "Who's Shirley?"

Victor grabbed the embroidered name patch over the left pocket of Ray's overalls.

"Oh, you mean this? She works with me at the store. She said that I can use her overalls if I wash them. She's pretty big, and she has a real good right hook, too."

Victor and Raymond laughed.

Ray turned back under the truck and asked, "What are you in town for? Business or pleasure?"

"Pleasure. We've just returned from out of town, and Mom was watching the boys for us, so we are just visiting with the family for a couple of extra days. Ally's with Betty in Grandma's house. They are cleaning things up in there today."

Ray replied sarcastically, "Lucky us."

Vic mustered a half-smile.

Ray rolled back to look at him and replied, "Just pullin' your leg, bro. At least you come around to visit once in a while. No one comes by anymore. It's like a ghost town around here. Your mother and sisters and me seem to be the only ones that come by anymore."

Ray crawled out from under the truck and dusted himself off the best he could. He grabbed an old rag that had been tossed on the top of the engine and tried to clean his hands a little more. Then he shoved the rag into his back pocket and bent down to open the cooler. He grabbed a beer for himself and tossed a Coke to Victor.

"You'd better lay off the hard stuff, bro. I hear that that will put a good sized hole in you," Ray laughed. "Sorry Dude, I don't have any Twinkies; I ate the last one."

"Does your mother know you're drinking?" Victor asked.

Raymond wiped his mouth and burped, "Yeah, she bought me this."

Victor sat down next to Ray on the old wooden chair and adjusted the radio that sat behind him. The radio's reception wasn't the best, but they weren't in the best area to receive a good signal. KTNN from Window Rock was the only station that Raymond wanted to listen to. It brought back many memories for him and Victor as they sat and listened to the Navajo Radio Announcers speaking their language. Victor and Ray sipped their drinks and looked at the old truck.

"Have you got it started yet?" Victor asked, breaking the silence and leaning forward.

"Only in my dreams," Ray wiped his face with the back of his hand and forearm.

Ray leaned forward also, putting his forearms on his knees and looking at the truck, knowing it was more trouble than it was worth. Then he looked at Victor.

"We sure had a lot of fun in this truck when we were kids," Ray said with a smile. "Grandpa sure was a good man. I really miss him."

Victor, feeling a rush of emotion come over him, stood up and turned away to quickly wipe an unexpected tear. Clearing his throat he asked, "What can I do to help out The Blue Bucket?"

"Well, we are missing some of the original parts, but I think that some of them may be in Grandpa's hogan," Ray quietly replied, pointing with his lips toward the hogan.

"Let me go get them for you," Victor said as he started to walk toward the deserted hogan.

"Hey bro, don't go in there. You crazy?" Ray said forcefully, dropping his beer and quickly jumping up to grab Victor, but it was too late.

Ever since Grandpa passed away, the hogan had remained empty. No one wanted to go in for fear of bothering the dead spirits. Navajo tradition dictated that the hogan should have been burned down or demolished, but no one in the family wanted to do that.

Victor, unaffected by that tradition, replied, "I'll just look in to see if I can find anything," and continued closer toward the hogan.

Running up, Ray grabbed his shoulders and said, "*Yei ya!* You are not supposed to go in there! It's bad luck. The evil spirits, remember?"

Victor saw the fear in Ray's eyes and tried to calm his cousin. "It's okay; I'll be right back, and besides, it's high noon."

Ray stood back shaking his head and watched Victor walk to the entrance of the hogan. The wooden door was padlocked. The door had replaced the woven rug years ago – before Victor could remember.

Victor's eyes were fixed on the padlock, but he shook the door anyway. To his surprise the door's hardware rattled off the door and the lock fell on the ground. Victor kicked the metal out of the way and pushed on the door. The squeaky hinges creaked as if they would break. The door was hard to push open because of the sand that had accumulated behind it. The wind had blown the fine sand in through the small gaps in the walls and the eroding roof.

Victor forced the door open, and as soon as he could squeeze through the small opening he had created, he entered the hogan, and with his foot, freed the door of the pile of sand behind it and opened it wide. The extra bit of sun let in through the opened door startled a mouse, which ran behind a box.

The inside of the hogan looked smoky from the sand that had just been disrupted. Dust covered everything and there was a cobweb in every corner. The flat log ceiling was almost ready to give way. The smaller logs had rotted away and the adobe covering the top had fallen partially into the living space. Along one of the eight walls was a small cupboard, which held Grandpa's things. Two cots were butted head to head along two walls opposite the cupboard. One of the metal beds had been stripped bare, exposing the metal straps and small springs that had once held a thin mattress.

A small table and two broken chairs stood just next to the door. The roof around the chimney of the wood-burning stove in the middle of the room looked very unstable, and the entire structure, although old and dying, sparked Victor's thoughts of happier times. Victor saw some old parts under one of the cots. But knew they weren't what he was looking for. *Not the same make. Those were from Grandpa's Ford.*

Victor got down on his knees to look under the other cot. He patted the old army blanket still covering a small part of the old bed. The dust and sand that rose up made him cough and he got to his feet and ran to the door for fresher air. As Victor emerged from the hogan bent over, his hands on his knees, Ray who had been sitting on the tailgate of the truck finishing his beer, leaped off and yelled, "*Shi* (my) heart! You crazy Indun! I told you not to go in there!" Ray began to run toward Victor but stopped about ten feet short of the structure.

Victor waved that he was okay. And he reentered.

The sunlit room looked different the second time around and Victor saw new details. One object that caught his eye was an aged leather suitcase sitting at the end of one of the beds. He looked at the case like a child looking at a present, not knowing if he should open it. He bent down to lift it from its resting place. As if from out of nowhere, a gust of wind whipped

31

through the room and forcefully slammed the door shut. Outside, Victor heard the flap of large wings. *The owl?*

The force of the slam loosened an already crumbling piece of ceiling from its place and a sizeable chunk fell to the floor. The dust on the floor billowed up and rose high into the air filling the space again. Victor's heart stopped, and he quickly stood up and headed for the door but stopped himself in the middle of the room.

Could Ray be right?

A cold chill ran up his spine and after breathing deeply, he began to laugh, thinking himself foolish for being so frightened of the wind. Regaining his composure, he looked at the piece of roof that had just fallen. The hole it left glowed with the light from the sun, and Victor followed the light as it lit directly on an old leather suitcase just under the bed. After debating whether or not to touch it, he turned back to pick up the suitcase and set it on the metal government bed. He carefully opened it and looked at the Wrangler Jeans and old leather belt folded neatly inside. Digging deeper, he discovered some old papers, yellow and cracked with time, but he could still see the Union Pacific Railroad letterhead, dated 1951.

Feeling uncomfortable about searching through items that didn't belong to him, Victor closed the suitcase, gently placed it where he had found it, and rose to leave. As he turned toward the door another gust of wind swept through the room, picked up a bit of sand and whipped it around until the small sand devil disappeared next to the other bed. Victor's eyes were drawn toward the other suitcase under the bed, and he knelt down beside it to investigate further. Victor wiped his hand across the suitcase. The thick dust and dirt moved to reveal the old worn cover. He carefully lifted the lid to reveal the contents.

An old shoebox tied with leather straps sat on the top. The leather was old and brittle. The package had not been opened for a very long time. Victor gently tugged at the leather knots.

The straps, which had once held strong, had become small and shrunken and the knots were easily loosened. Inside the box were an old watch, a turquoise necklace and silver rings, some papers inside of a plastic bag, an old book, and an old metal tobacco box.

Grandpa's favorite tobacco, Victor thought as he picked up the box, hoping to be able to smell one of his memories of his grandfather. The box rattled, making Victor even more curious. He opened it and dumped the contents onto the top of the shoebox lid.

Medals? Victor tried to arrange the mass to more easily see the treasure.

These look like military medals. But whose?

Victor's attention moved toward the plastic bag. He put in his hand and pulled out a pile of letters and papers. Looking at the first folded paper, his interest heightened and he tried to find a place to sit.

Discharge Papers. 1946. United States Marines. Lee Benally!? Grandpa never told us that he was in the Marines.

Victor sat wondering at the relics he had just uncovered and wondered why he was the one to find it. He picked up the contents of the shoebox and gently placed everything back. As he moved the old book out of the way to make room for the papers, he was confused at what Grandpa would have done with a book. He had never known Grandpa to read. Grandpa's education had come from his father. Victor picked up the book and turned it over noticing the scratches on the back. The book looked as if it had seen better days and his curiosity was intensified as he opened the front cover.

> *To our friend Lee Benally,*
>
> *Thank you for your generosity in saving our lives. We hope we can somehow repay you. As a token of our appreciation we pray that this book may bless you always.*
>
> *Elder Anderson and Elder Smith*

A Book of Mormon? I didn't know Grandpa had this. I wonder why he never shared this with me.

He gently closed the book, and trying to keep up with his emotions, took the shoebox in his arms and carefully walked out of the hogan.

Ray, watching Victor emerge from the hogan, jumped off the tailgate and started choking on his beer. "Hey Indun, what are you doing?" he coughed. "That stuff is evil." But he was still intrigued enough to clear a way for Victor to place the things on the tailgate of the truck, but was careful not to touch any of the items.

"Now the truck will never start!" Ray groaned.

"Grandpa was in the Marines in World War II," Victor explained.

"What War?" Ray asked, his mind still on the items sitting on his truck tailgate. "He never...what do you mean?"

Victor walked past Ray and called out to Ally and Betty to come out of Grandma's house. Ally poked her head out of a window, "What are you yelling at?"

"Come take a look at what I found," he pleaded.

"Hold on Hon', we'll be right out," Ally replied.

"Betty, Vic wants us to look at something outside." Ally stood up and held quickly onto the back of the chair closest to her thinking she might be sick. *What is going on? I must be feeling light headed from the cleaning detergents.* "Where did the boys go?" she asked Betty.

Betty herded the boys out the door and smiled to herself as they tripped over one another clambering down the path and around the back of the house to the old willow. Betty's pride in her grandchildren was hard to mask. She loved this small pair and their two-year old antics. Alec and Christian had lighter hair and skin than her other grandchildren, but she favored them more because she didn't see them as much as the others.

Victor had arranged the medals on the tailgate. He and Ray were talking as Betty and Allison joined them.

"I didn't know anything about it. I was looking for parts for the truck. I found this stuff." Victor said.

Betty looked at the tailgate and stood quietly. "Victor, what is it?"

"I went into Grandpa's hogan and . . ."

She looked at the treasure on the tailgate. "Where did you find that?" Betty said cautiously. "I've been looking for that stuff for years."

Victor wanted to hear more. He could sense that his mother wanted to tell a little bit more, but the moment was broken by the boys' screaming and crying just off in the distance. Allison ran toward the boys to find them standing on top of a red anthill. She could tell by the way the boys were grabbing at their pants and legs that the ants had began to bite them. Betty quickly grabbed Alec and started pulling all his clothes off and she told Allison to do the same. The boys were screaming and crying as the red ants continued to bite and torment them.

"I'll fill up the tub," Betty said, and she hurried to the house.

Victor and Allison grabbed the boys to take their small ,naked and sore bodies into the bathroom.

Allison held tight to Alec as his sobbing seemed to quiet a bit from the excitement of the ordeal. Christian nuzzled his head into Victor's neck and occasionally made a small sniffing sound.

"I sure wish that hadn't happened," Allison said to Victor putting an arm in his. "I thought we had warned the boys better about those stupid anthills."

"Oh, Honey, they'll be fine, don't worry," Victor comforted.

Allison stopped, "I can take Christian in, you grab that stuff off the truck. I don't want that to get lost."

Victor nodded, and handed the small boy to Allison, who cradled his little body in her other arm. Both boys held on tightly to their mother's neck and the trio made their way around the corner.

"I told you to leave that stuff alone," said Raymond, who had stood watching the excitement. "You'll have bad luck."

Victor, still unaffected by Raymond's dire prophecy, carefully placed the items back in the shoebox, put everything under his arm, and made his way to the house.

5

The boys had a warm bath and Betty put some lotion on the ant bites. After eating dinner they all looked and felt very tired. Allison was also not feeling well, so she lay down on the bed in the corner of the room with the boys and their blankets. Victor watched with love as his little family lay together entwined in innocent sleep. Allison was his only love and he was amazed that he loved her more every day. The boys' small bodies nestled close to Allison.

Betty was just finishing up the last of the frybread. The small kitchen had running water, a luxury Grandma had enjoyed for only one year before she died.

Ray was outside cleaning up the mess they left, but he was careful not to touch the tailgate and left it open. He had decided to give up on the truck for the night.

Betty sat down at the table in the center of the small room with Victor and looked at her son's family lying on the bed. She was so proud of the things her son had accomplished in his life, but she was most pleased that he had found a mate to grow old with.

Your grandfather is proud of you, son.

"Victor, your *Ni masani* (your grandma) told me some things about your *Ni cheii* (your grandpa)," Betty said. "Your grandpa had a twin brother. He was very close to him. They were only in their teens during World War II. Your grandma said that grandpa's brother, his name was Charlie . . . ," she paused. "You see, grandpa's brother decided that he didn't want to be a medicine man like your grandpa so he decided that he wanted to go off and fight the war. Charlie was a Code Talker."

Victor stared at Betty. "Why didn't Grandpa say anything about this?"

"Grandpa was a very complicated man, and he was very traditional. Things of the world were unimportant to him. He felt that keeping our tradition and learning the Diné way of life was important. He wanted you to know about your family and your heritage, but it was hard for him to talk about that part of his life, so he didn't. He tried to talk only about the good things, like being in Harmony and the old stories about your ancestors. For some reason he kept it to himself, he didn't want to talk about his time as a soldier during the war. It was hard for your *Ni masani* to help him. For years after the war he had only nightmares. There were many ceremonies done for him by your great grandfather and it seemed to help. After you grandkids were born he seemed more content and at peace."

"Years ago, I think it was in the early seventies, when I was a dorm aid at Sanostee, the ladies would talk about their fathers being Code Talkers. They said that it used to be top secret. The ladies told me that my dad was a Code Talker, too, but when I asked my father about it he would deny it.

He would rather talk about the family and how they were doing. Such thoughts kept his mind busy. He loved hearing about all of his grandkids. That was most important to him. He hoped that you would never have to see what he saw and heard. That's what grandma used to say about what your grandpa would tell her all the time in private."

Victor stood up from the table and walked over to the box, stopped, looked at his mother and said, "So why did he join the Marines if he was so opposed to it?"

"On the day your grandpa died, grandma and I were here at the house. Your grandmother never cried, she just stood folding his clothes into his suitcase."

* * *

"Betty do you know how I met your father?" Mary asked.

"No, you have never told me about that," Betty replied.

"I was only fifteen or sixteen years old when I first saw your father in the early summer, we just finished planting corn. My sister and I were herding sheep," she looked in the direction of Wheatfield Lake and smiled.

* * *

"Rosie, get up, we need to get back home and I think we have rested enough." Mary said.

"I can hear some cattle coming over the ridge, we'd better get moving," Rosie agreed.

The two stood up and dusted each other off. Off in the distance they saw a man walking toward them. He was carrying a large bag and appeared to be dressed in a light green suit of some kind.

As he drew nearer, they recognized the man as Jimmy, their brother.

"Jimmy!" they yell in unison and began running toward him. Jimmy was dressed in his olive green Marine uniform and was carrying a duffle bag over his shoulder. He had been gone for years and his sisters had missed him terribly. His dark, chiseled face and black eyes looked worn and older. He was still wearing his Military haircut, and he looked totally out of place in his desert surroundings. Rosie and Mary kissed and hugged him, laughed and cried. Jimmy cried with joy.

His life over the last years had been very strange, and he had often longed for home and family.

"Where are our parents?" Jimmy asked.

"They had to fix the corral," Rosie said. "They will be back later."

They started to gather things up to head for home when a herd of cattle came over the hill to the water hole and their clumsy descent scattered Mary and Rosie's sheep. Angry, Mary picked up several stones and looked for a target. Lee and Charlie were on horseback and were bringing up the rear when the sharp rocks started to hail down on them. Lee, looking up to see where the assault was coming from, set eyes on Mary. He stopped and stared at the most beautiful sight he had ever beheld. Mary's raw determination and anger did not deter Lee's gaze, and he was hypnotized until a sharp rock struck his left arm. The pain broke Lee's spell and he grabbed at his bleeding wound. Even the pain in his arm could not wipe the smile off his face.

Rosie had Charlie in her sights and was about to throw a large rock toward him when Jimmy stopped her.

"Wait, that's Lee and Charlie, I know them," Jimmy yelled. "Stop!"

Mary and Rosie stopped their attack reluctantly and looked at Jimmy, who ran up to greet his friends. Lee and Charlie got off their horses. Jimmy shook the twins' hands and they walked toward the girls.

Mary was in no way embarrassed by her assault on the two trouble makers and made it known that the twins had really made a lot of work for them. But Rosie turned red and looked away.

Lee looked at Mary and smiled shyly at her but Mary, still angry, glared at the handsome young man. The long sleeve of his cotton shirt was soaked with blood and Mary, angry that he seemed not to be bothered by the mess he was making, tore a piece of a flour sack that had held her lunch, walked over to Lee, and roughly tied the piece of cloth around his arm.

Lee's smile continued, and Charlie, also taking notice of Mary's beauty, watched in envy, wishing that Mary had chosen to hit him first.

Lee said in a low voice, "Sorry about your sheep."

"I will help you get your sheep gathered up," Charlie said.

"I'll help too," Lee replied.

Mary softened just a bit, "Does it still hurt?"

Charlie took Lee aside, "If we aren't back on time, Father will be angry. I think you should go ahead and I will come home later. Just tell Father where I am."

Lee agreed that someone should go back, but he thought it should be Charlie. Still, he reluctantly agreed and prepared to leave.

"It is good to see you again, Jimmy, I hope you can tell me stories of your adventures soon. Thank you again, Mary." Lee smiled and walked to *So'Doo Nidizini*, mounted, and rode off.

Charlie and the others help gather the sheep and put them in the corral.

"Yeah, Charlie why don't you stay for dinner?" Jimmy asked.

"Will you tell me stories about the war?" Charlie asked.

"Sure," Jimmy patted Charlie on the back and they walked toward the hogan.

"You have grown a lot since the last time I saw you," Jimmy said.

After the meal everyone sat around Jimmy and waited for his story.

Mary and Rosie kept their eyes glued to their older brother. They tried to memorize every feature of the man sitting before them.

"Start from the beginning." Rosie chimed.

"Okay. After we were loaded on the buses in Shiprock, we traveled to Gallup and then to California. The *Bilagana* wanted us to speak Navajo. Charlie, remember when we got the whip at boarding school for speaking Navajo? Now they wanted to know our language and they wanted us to help them with our words."

41

Charlie chuckled, "Why do the *Bilagana* want you to speak Navajo?"

"I can't tell you what it was for, but the *Bilagana* men in the uniforms at Shiprock are always looking for Navajo men that can speak both English and Navajo."

"I speak better English than you do, Jimmy," Charlie teased.

Charlie's eyes became wide with excitement as Jimmy's stories unfolded. Jimmy's adventures had taken him to strange places with strange sights.

"I met people from New York, Ohio, and Florida," Jimmy said. "I have a friend from Georgia. He has dark skin, even darker than that guy we knew at school."

"You mean Billy Blue eyes?" Charlie questioned.

"Yeah, he wants to come to visit. And the Japanese, some called them Nips, looked a lot like us but they spoke a strange language."

"What did you do in the Marines?" Charlie asked.

There was silence from Jimmy. His head bowed and his face reflected many emotions.

"Let's talk about it another time."

"But am I too old to join the Marines? I think I'm of age."

"No, they said I was nineteen years old when I joined. I think that's about right."

"What happened to Nelson and those others that went with you?" Mary asked.

Jimmy very quietly whispered, "They didn't make it."

The silence was broken only by the sheep's bell outside and the crackling in the wood-burning stove. The coziness of the small hogan made the atmosphere very comfortable.

Charlie did not want to leave, but realized that it was late. He stood up and headed for the door. "I'd better get home. My father is going to be upset that I have stayed this long."

"It was good to see you again, Charlie. I will come over and see you in a few days. Tell your father that I am coming."

Charlie nodded. The two shook hands and said, *hagoonee* (Good-bye). Charlie headed back home.

* * *

"So that's how grandpa got the scar on his arm. He used to call it his battle wound," Victor laughed.

"Your grandmother told me that story for the first time that evening. She also told me more about your great uncle Charlie and how he got in trouble with your great grandfather when he returned home."

"Your grandfather never did want to join the Marines in the first place. He wanted to be a medicine man like his father," Betty said. "He also wanted Charlie to stay and not join the Marines. He begged his brother not to join, but he was going to go anyway."

Raymond stood and stretched. "I need to head on the old dusty trail back to Shiprock. My old lady is probably thinking that I'm downing a couple of cold ones with the boys," he said, breaking the mood.

Ray started to walk toward the door, but then turned around.

"He told me he got in a fight with a bear. He said they look real cute from a distance but you'd better not get them mad, or else. Then he showed me his arm." Ray grabbed his left arm.

Ray turned toward the door and turned on the lights. "Hey it's real dark in here," he said.

"Kill the lights, Ray," Victor yelled, annoyed.

"Just sit down. Don't you want to hear the rest of the story? It is really getting interesting," Victor said, almost whispering.

"My old lady . . ." Raymond quietly retorted. He didn't want to leave but he knew all too well how suspicious his wife was. Of course he never helped ease her suspicions by ever telling her the truth.

"Relax, your wife can wait. I'll talk to her. . . she still has her back problems?" Victor replied, with concern in his voice.

"Yeah . . . the doc said no heavy lifting or fighting. Good thing for me," Raymond said. He turned toward the refrigerator and opened the door. There was no more beer.

"Hey! Where's the beer? Who took the beer?" he turned, resting his right arm on the door, looking around to see if anyone was going to turn around and help him in his time of need.

"Ray, you drank the last one a long time ago. No one else here drinks so just turn off the lights and relax, bro." Victor wanted Raymond to sit down and shut up. Everyone sat around the table. The setting of the sun was almost complete, but the pink clouds still cast shadows on the walls inside the room from the trees.

Victor looked at his mother eyes. Her expression suggested that she didn't want to continue, but she knew that Victor would persist.

"It's getting late, son. Do you want to head to Ute Mountain?" Betty asked, hoping for "yes." She knew better, but added, "Tonight the Bingo jackpot is $3,000."

Victor ignored her request.

And I was feeling lucky, she sighed.

"Okay, then the story goes, that evening when your grandpa got back . . ."

Victor listened intently and got up and walked over to the window where there was a clear view of the hogan.

I can't believe that happened years ago. Grandpa, I wish I had known this.

"I'm listening Mom, keep going . . ."

* * *

Lee turned to Lucy. "Thanks for the dinner, Mother, I haven't had food like that for days."

"I want to talk to you about the owl I saw today," Lee added.

"Where is your brother?" Lucy asked.

Lee felt ignored.

"Your father knows that something is going on with your brother. He has had dreams about thunder and lightning, and he is very frightened for you two boys."

Lee was silent and he walked outside to his father. He could hear the crickets in the bushes under the night sky overflowing with bright stars.

"Father, Charlie will be home soon," Lee stated.

"He is coming, I know, but soon he will be gone," James said quietly. He lowered his head and put his hand on Lee's shoulder. Then he guided Lee back to the hogan.

Lee walked back, confused, but needing to be quiet so that his father could think. After a few moments of silence in the hogan, they heard the dogs bellowing, and a short time later Charlie entered.

Nothing was said for the rest of the evening.

The brothers looked at each other as their father slowly turned off the kerosene lamp. But Lee was brooding, afraid of the future, afraid for his brother.

What will become of him? I worry about him, was Lee's last thought before he fell into a restless sleep.

* * *

Smoke was rising into the air in an unfamiliar place. All that could be seen were flying machines and hundreds of thousands of men in uniforms running from the water onto land. The men were yelling amidst huge explosions all around. He put his hands over his ears . . .

* * *

Lee suddenly awoke. He sat up quickly; he was sweating and breathing heavily. He looked around to see if everything was all right. He looked over to see Charlie.

He's okay, Lee thought to himself.

He then looked over at his mother and father. Mother was asleep but he noticed that Father was not there. Lee got up to see where he was. He stepped out of the hogan and felt the brisk pre-dawn air. He stared at the sky. The stars were beginning to fade as the sky prepared for the sun.

I love this place. Lee rubbed his eyes and he turned to find his father. Scanning the area, he noticed him on the ridge. He started to walk up to him, and as He got closer called out, "Father?" His father didn't respond. Lee continued closer. His father, still without turning around, spoke:

"Son, come sit down with me. When I was your age your grandfather and I would sit at this same place and greet the morning sun." James turned to Lee and smiled.

Lee said nothing and smiled back. They sat for an hour with nothing being spoken, enjoying the beauty and peace they felt all around them.

James broke the silence, "Son, go get your brother and meet me at Big Bear."

Quickly, Lee jumped up and headed back to the hogan.

I wonder what he is going to tell us this time, he thought, curious.

"Brother, get up and come with me. Father wants to talk." He tried to pull him up off the ground.

"Okay, okay, let go of me." Charlie moaned as he struggled to his feet.

Mother walked into the hogan. She had just gathered the water for the morning.

"Where are you boys off to today?" she asked as she washed her hands in the washbasin.

"We are going into the mountains," Lee said excitedly.

"I think that he's going try to stop me from joining the white man's army," Charlie supposed, not wanting to go to see his father.

"Let's go," Lee said, heading out the door.

"The morning is beautiful," Lee said as he stopped and looked over the valley. He turned to hear Charlie's response.

Charlie didn't stop or respond; he kept walking. Lee ran to catch up with him.

"What's wrong if we want you to stay?" Lee asked, putting his hand on his brother's shoulder. Charlie shrugged off Lee's hand. Charlie stopped and turned to him, his eyes were filled with anger and confusion. He was starting to say something, but when he looked into his brother's eyes, he saw that his brother truly cared for him. He spun back around, turning his back to Lee.

"The last one to reach Father is going to have to clean the sheep corral," Charlie shouted as he turned back around, pushed Lee down, and started to run.

Lee caught himself from falling, grinned, and started in pursuit. Charlie had already run over the first ridge and, standing on a large boulder, he turned back to stop and yell. "Brother, do you need help?!" He jumped off the rock and sprinted down a grassy area beside a small stream. The stream fed a shallow river that emptied into Big Bear Lake.

Lee stood on the top of the big rock that his brother had just left. He watched Charlie, knowing that he couldn't possibly catch him now. Although slightly upset that his brother was winning, he was glad to see that he could still have fun with his brother, and he sensed that he might never see him like this again. He paused to look over the valley. The sky was now blue and the sun still was not completely up. Toward the west Lee observed some large dark clouds starting to billow. The lake below reflected the blue of the sky. Hundred-year-old Ponderosa pines surrounded the entire lake and Grey Mountains.

This is home. Why would anyone want to leave? Lee

thought as he jumped off the rock and jogged down the grassy hill. He looked up to see his friend the Bald Eagle flying right above him, swooping up and down as if to follow Lee.

"Not today friend. I'm not going fishing. Try the other side of the lake where the bears are. Maybe you can get lucky," he yelled to the Bald Eagle as if it understood. But the eagle still followed.

Lee smiled as he got near the meeting place. He noticed that Father and Charlie were talking, but as Lee approached, the conversation stopped. Lee looked into Charlie's eyes and noticed that they were red. Lee was curious, but he said nothing.

Trying to hide his emotions, Charlie said with a half-smile, "You must have gotten lost, Brother. Now I can enjoy watching you clean." he playfully pushed Lee.

Lee quickly pushed him back, "There is always tomorrow."

"I am glad that we can meet together as men," James interrupted, extending his arm and motioning for the boys to sit down.

The boys obeyed.

"The two of you are turning into men now," he began. Pointing to Lee's friend, Bald Eagle, he said; "I have been observing that eagle all morning. Sometimes I wish that I could be as free as that eagle. He is free to hunt. To travel, and to go wherever he chooses. But I want to tell you that freedom, even for the eagle, comes with a price. He knows that through mistakes and choices that he has made he continues to survive and enjoy the freedom. But he also knows of the unknown that one day may end his life, so he is cautious of his decisions. He only chooses what he can do."

He looked down at his boys. They were silent; they had never heard Father talk like this before.

"I want to tell you about the unknown which all men are

afraid of. For as long as our ancestors have entered into this fourth world, we have been afraid of the unknown. But I also fear for what I know. Follow me and I will tell you what our ancestors have known." He started to walk away along the lakeside.

Quickly the boys jumped up and followed.

"This is our land. We have been here for centuries. The other Indian tribes, the Spanish and the Mexicans tried to take this from us. Now our new white brothers say they are our new fathers. Our people now say, 'what will become of the Diné?' The white people give us the name Navajo, and this name is unknown.

"We live in a new unknown. Our neighbors are also confused what to do. They ask the same questions: what to do? Your grandfather was captured by the white army and sent to a prison across the Rio Grande. While he was in this prison, he also asked 'what will become of us?' He told me of this when I was your age. For centuries we have had difficult times, but still we live on."

As James surveyed the land around him he reverently continued, "All the answers of life are here." He swept his arm across the silent land.

The boys were puzzled. They looked around for the answer he indicated.

"No, sons the answers are everywhere," Father said, pointing to the flowers and trees and mountains.

"There is no unknown if you are in *Hozo* (harmony). Mother Earth and Father Sky have the answers. But it is within us to find the answers. If we choose to."

He picked up a handful of dirt and let it run through his hands. Then he turned to see if his sons understood. Being a patient man, he paused. He looked out to see the eagle swoop down to the lake to grab a fish, his talons extended out in front of his body. As he neared the water, his talons hit the water with lightning speed and his large wings began to beat powerfully to lift himself out of the water. The effort produced nothing.

"Try again brother." Lee said.

The three watched the eagle circle the lake for another run. He started down again, exactly repeating his attack. This time he came up with a fish.

The three cheered.

"Enjoy it," Lee said as the eagle flew off into the distance.

"I understand that I can't make both of you understand this in one day just like the eagle can't learn to hunt like that in one day," James said. " It takes time, but I will teach you all I know. Come."

They started to walk again.

"The unknown is what men do not understand, refuse to understand, or just can't understand. Normal men never use what is given to them. Sometimes they only hear with their ears, only see with their eyes, only feel with a touch. They forget to use their hearts and minds; they forget to listen. As a holy man, I have learned that if you use your heart and mind when something is put in front of you, there is no unknown. The choices that are present everywhere require understanding. For me, I know that all the choices already have been answered so there shouldn't be any questions. Right?" He turned to Charlie.

Charlie, not knowing to what say, said nothing, but looked away.

Lee noticed the uncomfortable silence and broke in quickly, hoping to understand. "Father, so if I'm in harmony, will I know the future? The choices already have an answer?"

"For every decision that one makes there is an outcome. But some people don't know the outcome. That is the unknown that almost everyone is afraid of."

"Father, do you know our future?" Lee asked, almost hoping he wouldn't answer.

There is a pause. The seconds passed like hours before Father began to answer the question.

"Yes, I do know the answers. But you have the choice to choose the right one."

Lee noticed that his Father didn't look at Charlie.

James felt his throat tightening. His eyes began to water and the pain almost overwhelmed him. He staggered.

Charlie noticed his father's pain but said nothing.

Lee, concerned, but more confused, asked, "Father, are you okay?"

"Yes, I'm okay. I just wanted to tell you both to be aware of your senses like your four-legged brother the bear and mountain lion and our friend the eagle. You are not yet aware of this. We will study the bear, mountain lion and eagle; then we will move onto the others," he said, trying not to let his emotions overtake him again. Noticing the wind moving in, he asked, "Boys, do you notice the wind? What is it telling you?"

Lee quickly answered, "I noticed that same wind days ago. It's going to rain and it feels like it's going to be a big storm, too."

"Yes, but what else?" James urged.

"I . . . don't know what else," Lee said, trying to find an answer.

James waited patiently.

"Change!" Charlie answered. "The rain changes the land, giving it life. It changes the landscape by moving the earth. The water brings life but sometimes it can...take a life."

"Good Charlie. The rain brings change. It brings life that wasn't there before and it can also take life," James agreed.

"So, even you can't know the future of everything," Charlie said confidently.

"Yes, you are right son, but there is no unknown within me. I know what is a part of me and that is the both of you."

James knew Charlie was still upset.

"I know that you are my sons. The both of you are all that your mother and I have to pass on our tradition. I hope the both of you understand that. Many of your ancestors have sacrificed their lives so that our life can be possible. If I teach you nothing more, remember that." James noticed the skies getting darker.

"Come on, let's go home and see what your mother has for us." James followed behind the twins, praying silently, *Oh great one, please make Charlie understand this. I fear for him.*

"Brother, are you still going to join this army?" Lee asked in a light whisper, hoping that Charlie might have reconsidered.

Charlie turned to Lee and said, firmly, "I have to do this. It is what I want to do, you have to understand."

"I don't understand . . . why is it so important for you to go and fight this war that we have no business being in?" Lee whispered.

Charlie stopped and stared into Lee's eyes: "I read to you almost every night in that book. Although I don't agree with it, you said you like the way it makes you feel. I have asked you before why this book is so important to you and you said you don't know. It is the same thing for me. I need to go. I want to go. I just have to find out for myself why. I don't have an answer for you, but promise me, brother. . .if something happens to me that you will finish what I have started. I know that you need to go, too. There is something we must learn about this war. I can't explain what it is. I just know it. Promise me, please."

Lee, moved by his brother's fervent plea, replied, "Yes, I will promise you."

Charlie added, "This book is our promise. Keep the book

near you and if anything should happen to me this book will comfort you."

"Nothing is going to go wrong, Brother. You will go and you will come back and we will keep reading the book," Lee said, trying to convince himself that nothing would happen. A part of him knew that this would be the last time he would see Charlie.

They continued their journey back home. That evening the storm pounded down on the small home. The horses sought shelter in their small corral, while the dogs hid under anything they could find.

"The storm is strong. It is bringing much change this time . . ." a deafening crack of thunder interrupted James. Everyone braced for the next one.

"It's getting closer," Lee remarked.

"Yes, there is going to . . ."

Rolling thunder and lightning struck near the home and sent a veil of dust through the room, Shaking the small structure. After a few more moments...

"It's leaving now. You boys go check on the horses and I will check on the sheep," James said as he started for the sheep corral. The twins headed for the horses, which seemed to be okay, unfazed by the lightning and the light rain. Lee and Charlie both watched the clouds and heard the thunder rolling toward Shiprock.

"I love the smell after the rain. The wet trees and bushes smell so good," Lee said, lifting his head to the breeze.

Charlie also breathed deeply and they both sat on the wooden corral trying to keep their balance on the wet wood.

"Look, you can see the stars now. And look at those falling stars and look over there, at that cluster of stars. Do you see it?" Lee asked.

"Of course, but look over there at the brightest one

surrounded by the all the little ones," Charlie replied.

"We should ask father to tell us about the coyote and how he put the stars in the sky. The Big Dipper, and the seven sisters and how he just threw all the stars up when he got tired of the job," Lee said.

Back in the doorway of the hogan, James and Lucy stood observing their twins.

Already knowing the answer, Lucy asked, "Does he still want to go?"

"I don't understand why. I will begin the warring ceremony tomorrow. Is everyone still coming?" James turns to Lucy, his eyes wet but not from the rain.

Lucy gently grabbed his right arm and leaned her head on him as they continued to watch their twins until they headed back to the hogan. In a few minutes the kerosene lamp hummed in the corner where the twins slept. Charlie was reading to Lee, a nightly event. Suddenly, Charlie stopped, "Those Gamalii (Mormons) sure can tell a story."

James interrupted, "What were the names of those boys again?"

Charlie turned to the front cover to read the inscription, "Elder Anderson and Elder Smith."

"The one with white hair was the one that got sick last winter . . . or was it the one with brown hair?" Charlie asked.

"I don't know. They both look the same, anyway," Lee laughed.

"It was the one with the white hair. His feet were almost frozen off and his nose too," James recalled, concerned.

"It is incredible to see these two boys sacrifice their lives for their belief. I really enjoy their book. They were friendly young men," James said.

"I really wanted those two to stay a little longer. I wonder what happened to them?" Lee mused.

There was moment of wonder in the small room. Then the silence was broken.

"Brother!" Charlie interrupted, "do you want me to read or not?"

"Yes, go ahead," Lee laughed.

"Charlie, the ceremony starts tomorrow for your journey," James added before he fell asleep.

.

6

"Brother, I will miss you," Lee said, clearly trying to avoid bringing his emotions to the surface.

"I will miss you, too, Lee. When I return we will finish the book; remember to take care of the book and let it be a good memory of me," Charlie said, trying to hold back his tears. He quickly turned to his parents.

"Son, I wish you a good journey and don't let them change you too much," James said as he held his son's shoulders.

"Son, make sure that you remember your home," Lucy said with tears in her eyes.

"I will miss you all and will never forget who I am," Charlie said and turned to walk down the dirt road to Shiprock.

* * *

"So what happened to Charlie?" Victor said impatiently.

"Son, it's getting late and I'm getting tired. Can we finish this tomorrow?" Betty asked, starting for the door.

"But mom, just a little longer?" Victor pleaded.

"It's 2:30 in the morning, son," Betty said, stifling a yawn.

"Okay, okay," Victor moaned and walked Betty to her truck outside.

The sky was covered with stars and the air was brisk and clean. Both Betty and Victor enjoyed the calming effect of the quiet night. They stood for a moment and breathed in the fresh air.

"I'll be up in the morning to cook you guys breakfast," Betty smiled wearily.

"Okay, Mom; then you have to the finish the stories, all right?" Victor gave Betty a hug.

He watched her drive off until he could no longer see the tail lights of her truck. He felt something behind him and he quickly turned around to see what was there . . . but there was nothing. He looked at the trees and listened to the crickets and felt a slight breeze . . . but nothing else. He slowly turned toward the large Globe Willow tree that was over fifty-years old.

Looking closer he noticed a white owl staring down at him. The full moon lit up the night and the owl sat perched, large and imposing, as if he wanted to be seen by Victor.

"Well, you have me now don't you," Victor said, not sure if he should ignore or talk to the owl. The owl hooted as if he were speaking, and then flew off into the darkness.

"Well that was weird," Victor said, confused and bewildered.

He then yelled after the owl, "What is that supposed to mean?"

After waiting a moment for an answer, Victor shrugged his shoulders and walked back into the house.

"He's a messenger," Ray said with his eyes still shut. He was slouched over in an old vinyl recliner that was held together in places with Duct Tape.

"What?" Victor asked.

"Do you remember that we used to be scared of the owls?" Ray mumbled. "Grandpa would always say that we needed to come inside the house after dark or else the owls would come down and bite our ears off." Ray sat up in the chair.

"Oh yeah, I remember now," Victor chuckled.

"You know after you left on your church mission or wherever you went...where did you go Swasiland? Sweden? oh anyway Grandpa told me that he wanted you to be the next medicine man. I wanted the job but Grandpa said that I had no discipline." Ray stared off and was thinking, *I really wanted the job I guess I drink too much, and he was right about the discipline. But why Victor? He has no interest.*

"Hey Ray, but what does that have to do with an owl," Victor asked, confused.

Ray groaned as he got up and headed over to the dirty washbasin. He looked down at the brown water and grabbed a handful of it and splashed it over his face. He felt like a new man. He reached over to grab a torn rag and wiped his face. He turned to find Victor.

"The owl is the messenger of good news. That's what Grandpa said," Ray said, sitting back down on his chair, and trying to find his comfortable spot again. Then he smiled. "I'm staying the night, I had too many beers and I don't want to see my lady tonight and I don't feel like getting beat up. Good night, bro. We'll talk later when I can remember what I'm saying." He slowly went to sleep.

Victor looked around the room. Everyone was asleep. He walked over to the bed and covered the twins with a blanket. He leaned over and kissed the twins and Allison, who stirred.

"Vic honey what time is it?" she slurred, wiping her eyes and looking at her watch.

3:15 a.m.

"Vic, don't you ever go to sleep like normal people? It's late and the sun will be coming up in a couple of hours," she lay back down.

"Well, honey, I'm so wired I can't sleep. You know this is the first time I've heard about all this," he said, sitting down next to her.

"That's nice hon....," she drifted back into sleep again.

Victor pondered the years spent with his grandfather and he tried to remember if there were any hints of what he had heard this evening. The only time he thought there might be something. . .

I can't believe that all these years I didn't even know that Grandpa had this life. I . . .

* * *

"Victor, I want to tell you about my an experience I had when I was your age. . ."

Victor quickly interrupted, "Look, Grandpa... did you see that? I can't believe that bear is just sitting there on the edge of the river waiting for the fish."

"Vic, you've been gone too long. You have been away from your home and you are forgetting where you came from." Lee looked at Victor, a little disappointed that his grandson had forgotten the simplest of activities that happened there.

"I know, but it's so nice to see the wildlife again. In a few weeks I'll be heading on my church mission." Victor slowly breathed in the fresh air. "I am really excited to leave. I have never been outside the country. I can't believe I'm heading to Switzerland, and for two years...wow," Victor said with excitement.

"Have you ever been outside the country, Grandpa?" Victor asked, and then felt foolish that he had even proposed such an absurd notion.

I think that Grandpa could never leave the country. He would probably be too scared to leave here, anyway.

"There was a time that I thought it would be interesting in traveling away from here," Lee answered, looking away from Victor as his emotions quickly rose to the surface. "Victor, I'm happy that you are able to leave and learn more about the world. It will make you appreciate this place even more. I wanted to tell you a little about my experience that I had. I had to leave this place for a short while. It was an important journey just like yours is going to be. I had made a decision and I had to promise myself and my father that I would never forget who I am. Your great grandfather told me that I needed to know and learn the way of the Diné. I believe that your purpose is to know the difference between the white man's religion and our religion. I have nothing against the Gamalii (Mormons). They are good people. I want you to listen to our ancestors and know that you will never forget them. I truly believe that you will know our traditions in the near future, so listen. I will be here when you return from your journey," Lee smiled at Victor and looked back at the bear and her cubs feasting on fish.

"Don't worry about me, I will always remember you Grandpa," Victor replied with confidence.

"I don't think I could ever forget this place. I heard all of the stories and the stories of when you were my age. It can't be so much different, right Grandpa?" he smiled.

"No, Victor, my teenage years were spent doing things that I hope you never have to experience." Lee put his hands on Victor's shoulder.

"Come, let's go home. I'll have to tell you about that later, and maybe I'll show you my blue book. You know that book from your white man's church?"

"Tell me Grandpa. I haven't heard this story yet. You mean that you had the missionaries teach?" Victor said, excited by the possibility.

"It was the winter time. . ."

* * *

"Victor wake up! It is 9:00 a.m.," Allison said. "You were talking in your sleep again."

Victor looked at her as though she were a stranger; not quite aware he was awake. He quickly got up and looked around to familiarize himself with the room.

His hair was pointing in every direction but down.

"Hey bro, I didn't know that you talk in your sleep. You were talking about bears or beers or something. Anyway, I'd better get going; my old lady is probably throwing out my clothes again," he gulped his coffee.

"I gotta go gang, I'll see you later. I want to hear more about Gramps and his adventures." He slowly walked out and slipped a little.

"@#%$!% My head...sorry you had to hear that, Allison." Ray said as the door shut.

Allison laughed at Ray and shook her head in disapproval. Then she turned to Victor, but Victor seemed to be somewhere else.

"Hey, are you. . ."

"My dream I had about my Grandfather. . ." Victor stood up and looked around at the twins playing on the floor.

Allison looked concerned and stepped closer.

"My dream. He was going to tell me about his past and he wanted to tell me. . ." He sat back down.

"He wanted me to know about it and he was going to tell me. He was going to tell me. I can't believe I didn't listen."

"Morning everybody." Betty entered the small house with a bag of groceries and a pan containing breakfast. She set her bundles on the table and looked over at Victor.

"Son, what's wrong? Are you ok?"

He looked up at his mother.

"Victor, you need to brush your hair," Betty said.

Betty and Allison laughed.

"What?"

"You look terrible," Betty said. "I have some breakfast I made this morning." She picked up one of the boys and Allison picked up the other. They sat at the table and Betty uncovered the pan which contained Victor's favorite breakfast, Nanescadi, eggs, potatoes–and Coke.

When the delicious smell hit Victor's nose he was suddenly fully awake. He sat down with everyone.

"I told you, Allison, Victor never says that he isn't hungry,"

Betty said as she started to clean up around the house. Allison stood up to help Betty.

"No, no, sit. I already ate this morning," Betty said gently pushing Allison down to sit with her family. Betty reached into her pocket and took out a Marksmanship medal.

"Your Grandpa was a great shot," she said to all of them, but looking at Victor. "I found this earlier this morning when I was looking through some things your Grandma gave me."

"Tell us more, Mom. You seem to know everything," Victor said, hoping she would stay in one place and stop for a minute.

"Okay, let me clean this bowl," she said and sat at the table.

She took a deep breath and started; "Grandma said that Grandpa never wanted to go to fight against the Japanese until your uncle. . ."

* * *

"The storm is loud again," Lee said, trying to make conversation.

The silence in the hogan was deafening.

"Father, it's like the same storm we had when Charlie was here..." As soon as he said it he knew he shouldn't have. He looked down at the floor and began making circles in the dirt with a walking stick.

I wonder what Charlie is doing right now?

* * *

"Hey, private, do you believe this weather? All we see here is rain and more rain," Thomas said.

"Hey chief, what's HQ wanting us to do now? Sit and wait until we get killed?" snapped O'Reilly, sticking another Lucky Strike in his mouth.

Charlie didn't answer but started to wind up his radio for power. Mortar fire seemed to be getting closer but the destruction still sounded far away. He could barely see from his foxhole, but the setting sun looked red through the black and gray smoke. As he looked at his buddies huddled together for warmth, he tried to enjoy a small moment. The smell of death and hot metal seemed to be all around.

I can't get used to all of this.

Charlie picked up the radio receiver and spoke in Navajo, "HQ HQ this is 'frybread.'" he was trying to joke with the other Navajo off shore on the battleship.

"Hey you're going to get in trouble," the other code talker responded.

"Who is going to understand this anyway?" Charlie replied.

Charlie noticed a strange silence in the air; and he set his radio down to clear the sweat from his forehead and stepped back to look up at the sky. The night sky had cleared enough that he could finally see the stars.

Just like home. I love to watch the stars.

The sky was the only familiar part of Charlie's very different life, and for a moment he lost himself in the vast expanse of sky.

He heard a whistling sound that pierced the night. Almost as if in slow motion, Charlie turned around and saw his friends trying to run for cover. As he turned back he felt a quiet calm and then he saw a . . . bright, white flash.

* * *

The thunder woke up Lee. He felt a sharp pain in his stomach and he knew something was wrong.

Charlie...Charlie.

Lee quickly got up. He noticed that his father was gone. He stepped out in the cool morning air. He heard the faint sounds of singing in the distance. *Father?* He slowly approached so as not to disturb him.

James sat with his back to Lee; as Lee approached, James stopped singing but didn't turn around.

"I had a bad dream about Charlie. I couldn't go back to

sleep," Lee started.

"Your brother is dead. . . it was no dream. It was his spirit telling you that he is in another place," James said quietly.

Lee shook his head–no! But he knew his father was right. His eyes began to water. He wanted to be tough and not show any emotion, but as his father stood up and turned around, Lee could see that he had been crying, too. He stepped closer to Lee and they embraced each other.

Lee still fought against the reality of his father's words.

After a long moment, Lee stammered, "Does Mother know?"

"Yes, she knew before I did."

James started back to the hogan.

7

Two months passed.

The last horse and rider could be seen leaving a trail of dust on the red sandy road. The Ceremony had gathered many men from across the valley. James and Lucy felt the blessing was necessary for their son.

Lee had gathered his belongings in a small woven bag that his mother had made. He put the bag over his shoulder and turned to his parents.

"I don't think you should go. Your brother is dead and your father wants to teach you the way of our tradition," Lucy paused, overcome by emotion. "You are the only one left. There is no one else to pass this on to. Your father is worried about your decision to go," She paused again and looked into her son's eyes and smiled.

"You are my only son now. Please. . ." she stopped and wiped her eyes, but stepped away, knowing that the decision had already been made.

"Mother, I know that I'm needed here to learn the Wind Way of our family. I know that it is important. But when Charlie was here he was teaching me English. He told me that there was something we had to know. I'm beginning to feel that too. I know I need to do this. I have to finish what he started and fight for him and for our white brothers." Lee put his hands on his mother's shoulders. I know it is hard to explain but I need to do this. I have spoken to Father and I have promised him that I will never forget our tradition and that I will be a medicine man like him and Grandfather. I promise I will return, mother." He put his arms around her and thought, *I wish I could better explain this. I hope she will one day know that this is the right decision.*

Lucy cried, but as she held her son, she was comforted by his strength. Lee and Charlie had grown into two different men. Lee had been so much like his father; quiet, thoughtful and in touch with the earth around him. Charlie had always been the one they had to look out for. He found pleasure in playing jokes on the family and his friends. Lucy also felt a quiet comfort in the ceremony that would help Lee on his journey.

Lee smiled at his mother and she saw how much he looked like his father. He turned to his father.

"The ceremony will help you on your journey. I know that you will return." James said, knowing the truth of his words. James handed Lee his Medicine Man pouch. Lee handled the pouch with care. Such a sacred and important article demanded complete care.

Lee looked at his father with a questioning stare and said, "But father, I can't take this."

"You will need this to help you and to give you strength," James said.

Saying nothing, Lee looked at his parents and started his journey to Shiprock.

Though the sun was beating down on him, he was undeterred, and as he jogged, thoughts of his brother kept him company.

Brother, I know that you are with me. I have our blue book to keep us company. I'm scared but I know that if I keep this near me you will protect me too. Remember, brother, the times we would run down this trail all day and chase rabbits? What fun did we ever find in chasing rabbits, anyway? I don't know. But it was fun. Remember this place by the Black Thumb Sticking Up. There is water. Yes. Water. I need some water but not too much. he thought, looking to see if the place was still there. *Yes, there–just behind that cedar tree.*

After he drank, he sat and looked at the blue sky. There was not a cloud present. He looked back at his home. He could barely see the place.

I hope I can come back. I don't want to disappoint Father. I need to stay alive. Right, brother, I will stay alive.

He continued his journey. It was almost evening as he entered Shiprock. The smell of fry bread was in the air.

I'm near. I can smell mutton and fry bread.

As he walked among the hogans, he was able to pick out the different smells lingering close to the separate dwellings – Tobacco and beer mingled with the heaviness of greasy frybread:

He walked toward a number of fires in the distance surrounding a couple of large buildings and tents. He took a deep breath and headed to the fire where two men dressed as priests, were standing. There was a large black car parked next to the building.

Wow, that sure is a big black wagon with no horses, Lee said to himself.

"Good evening young man are you looking. . ." the Priest asked. Lee quickly turned around.

"Good heavens, young man I didn't mean to startle you. I was saying, are you looking for a place to stay?"

Silence.

"Are you a student looking for a place to stay?"

Silence.

"Are you a student?" the Priest repeated.

Lee mustered together some words and replied, "Y. . .yes, I am student. I need to go school here."

I hope he understood what I just said.

The priest smiled and led him gently by the arm to the church and motioned him to an empty corner of the room. Lee walked to the corner and set his things on the floor. The priest left and came back with a thin blanket and Lee settled in for a good night's sleep.

The next morning, Lee got up off the dirt floor. The sun shone through the window and the aroma of coffee filled the air.

I need to find out if someone can tell me about joining the army. It's been a long time since I've been here. It looks like nothing has really changed.

Lee walked along the outside of a few buildings until he came across a small building with *Shiprock Camp School* on a sign over the door. He slowly entered the small area, hoping that he wouldn't disrupt the class. As he scanned the room, he noticed a few familiar faces. He slowly took off his straw hat and held it with his two hands so as not to draw too much attention to himself, but it was too late; the whole class turned to look.

"Good morning young man; you're welcome to come and join us if you're interested. Today we're learning about the world. . . ," the teacher explained.

Their attention quickly moved past Lee to two men in uniform who entered behind him. Lee also turned to see the men in uniforms just like the one Jimmy was wearing that day at Wheatfield Lake. The neatly pressed shirts and pants and shiny black shoes caught Lee's attention. As the tall men entered the room, Lee immediately noticed an unfamiliar smell.

What is that smell coming from their faces? It's making me dizzy, he thought.

"Sorry for the interruption, ma'am. We're with the United States Marines and we are looking for new recruits to join," the taller of the two said.

"We are looking to see how old your class is to see how many can be drafted. Do you know if there are any young men that are eighteen years old?" the shorter one asked.

Lee noticed that they were talking about being eighteen years old.

I think I'm nineteen years old. I was told I was born in the fourth season and I think it has been eighteen or nineteen seasons ago. I should be old enough.

"Of course, let's see, I think only a few of my students are eighteen years old. It's so hard to know how old they are. They don't keep a record of their ages around, so we just have to guess sometimes. But most of them we can tell. But you never know." She gave a half smile.

"Uh, students, how many of you think you are eighteen years old?" she paused: No one answered.

"These men want to know how many of you are old enough to join the army," She said as she took off her glasses.

Suddenly, to Lee's surprise, all the young men in the room raised their hands with excitement. He noticed that half of them were not even eighteen years old. They were only fifteen years old, but he wasn't going to say anything.

"There will be a bus tomorrow that will be heading into Gallup in the morning. So if you are eighteen years old, we want you on that bus," the taller one said. They put their hats back on and headed out the door.

"Well thank you for coming, gentlemen," the teacher said. "I can't believe there aren't enough men anywhere else on the reservation," she said, quietly voicing her disapproval of war. "I can't believe you have to take my class." She softly cleared her throat and turned toward Lee.

"I'm so sorry that you are still standing there. You can have that chair there." She pointed to the last chair by the wall.

Lee sat down behind a friend he knew from Lukachukai, which was just over the mountain from Red Valley. The boy in front of him slowly turned his head. "So, you're going to join the army too, like your brother? By the way, how is he doing, anyway? I guess that he has been gone for almost two summers now."

Lee didn't respond.

"Excuse me you two. You know the rules. No speaking Navajo in here. Only English." She tried to be nice.

These Indians are never going to speak proper English. They are going to be the death of me, she seemed to be thinking. "Now let's begin again."

Lee's friend turned back in his chair after the teacher turned to the chalkboard.

"I'm going to tell them that I'm eighteen years old so that I can join. I want leave this place. We just sit here each week and she thinks that we don't understand English. She says the same thing over and over again. I'll show you, watch this."

The young man raised his hand in the air.

"Yes, Walter?" the teacher stopped.

"Miss Peterson I don't understand what you said. Can you start over?" Walter said, confusion written all over his face.

Miss Peterson's face started to turn red. She had just spent almost an hour going over the history of Germany and where it was located.

Walter leaned back on his chair and whispered loud enough for Lee to hear. "Lee, this is our favorite part—when her face changes color and she walks around mumbling to herself. This is the only fun we have."

Miss Peterson stepped from around her desk and tried not to explode. She calmly put down the book, and looked up at the blank eyes that stared at her.

"How many of you want me to start over? Wait, wait how many of you did not understand me." She hoped that no one would raise their hand, but everyone in the room raised their hand.

"I. . .I. . .I. . . am going to go outside for a moment to smoke a cigarette. And when I return we will go over this until you all understand me. . ." Silence. "Understand?"

Still no response.

She walked quickly and deliberately out of the room with her purse in her hands.

"There she goes again," smiled Walter.

Half the class chuckled and the students relaxed.

"How are your parents in Red? Are they okay with you leaving? My father said that your father is a good Medicine Man. You are going to be the next. I think that is good. We always need good holy men. Me, I want to play too much. You know, joke around." He slapped Lee on the shoulder.

Lee wasn't in the mood to talk. His thoughts were on the mission at hand. He smiled back at Walter as the teacher entered the room.

8

The next morning Lee was the first in line waiting for the bus to arrive.

The bus drove in from Farmington, It looked like a large silver bullet. Lee noticed that his stomach was getting tighter and his palms were getting wet. But he didn't want anybody to notice. Everyone was introducing themselves to each other as the bus began to fill. As the bus doors closed, everyone quieted down for the journey to Gallup as a white man started to prepare them for what was to come.

"First of all, you fellas are all going to have a physical, and if you pass you'll be headin' to California for basic training. The rest of you will have to go home or back to boarding school. Understand?" The man spit out a mouthful of chew on the bus floor.

The Navajo men on the bus all nodded their heads.

The man smiled a half smile to himself as if to say, *Most of these boys don't know what they are getting themselves into. But anything could be better than boarding school and farming.*

They sat in their own thoughts, thinking about what lay ahead. But no one spoke. The bus passed Sheep Spring trading post and Lee looked out the bus window at the small store. *I have never been this far from home.* He continued to look back at the store until it disappeared behind a hill. After what seemed a short time, the bus arrived at Gallup. The city looked bigger than any city Lee had ever seen and he stepped out of the bus and looked around.

Wow, there are white people everywhere and cars and trains.

Lee and the other men were unsure of where to go, but the crowd slowly moved closer to where a soldier, holding a clipboard, was yelling, "All right boys, those that are here for the armed forces. . .," he pointed to a group of white men, "stand over there."

The crowd walked over to the men.

"OK, first of all, all of you need to get back on this bus. You will be instructed by this person here. His name is Sergeant Frances. He will be your friend for the next twenty-four hours. So let's move out!" the man yelled.

Everyone crowded onto the other bus. Before they could even get comfortable, the trip was over.

"Everyone off the bus. Now move it. What are you waiting for, a special invitation?" Sergeant Frances yelled.

Everyone got off the bus and headed into a room of what appeared to be a hospital. Sergeant Frances stood at the front of the room, "I need two lines right here," he said, pointing at two areas directly in front of him. Lee quickly picked a line and stood quietly.

"Now boys, take off all your clothes and wait while these fine men in the white uniforms take you in these rooms and give you your physical," Sergeant Frances ordered as he paced between the two lines.

Everyone took off their clothes and stood with all they owned in their arms. Lee looked around and only counted five Navajo brothers in a room of thirty. Another man entered the room and picked out the Navajo Men one by one and ordered them to stand in front of him. "Are you an Indian?" the man asked.

"No sir, I am Navajo. We are all Navajo," Lee replied.

The man looked at him and said nothing. He then looked at the four others and turned, "All right, men, follow me." He marched them into a separate room with hard shiny floors and shiny chairs along the walls.

There was a table closer to the middle of the room with a white curtain drawn halfway around it. One of the men in white picked Curtis Yazzie out of the group and motioned him to come beside the table and the curtain was pulled.

I'm glad they didn't pick me, Lee thought. His feet were cold and he was getting tired of standing. Two of Lee's friends were called behind the curtain and didn't return. A man then called Lee back, gave him a physical, and then led him out the door and down a hall to another room. This room had several tall chairs that were lined up in front of a large mirror; each chair had a man sitting in it with a large cloth around his neck. Next to each chair stood a man with some sort of machine in his hand. Lee had never seen anything like it. He watched with fascination as the man with the machine in his hand, would shave the hair off of the heads of the men, leaving a gray scalp in its place. The floor below the chair was swept clean and as quickly as one man left another was seated in his place. Lee sat down in a vacant chair and he watched almost sadly as the man with the razor quickly removed hair that had never been cut before. *This must be what our sheep feel like,* Lee thought as clumps of his hair fell to the floor. After he was dismissed from the barber's chair, Lee was taken to the showers. Although not totally foreign, the showers were always a unique experience.

The group was then ushered into another room. Lee had been taught by his father to use his sense of smell as readily as he used his sense of sight and Lee's nose was making his mind whirl with new smells that he had not experienced before. The smell of hot food was a welcome smell. A smell not as welcomed was the smell of the big white man in front of him who smelled of cow manure. It was obvious that he had not yet been taken to the showers.

I wonder where he is from? Lee thought.

As the line got closer to the table, and as the man in front of

Lee reached the table, one of the man behind the desk asked, "What's your name, son?"

"Billy Joe Douglas, sir," the Cowboy replied.

"Where are you from, Mack?" was the next question.

"Oklahoma. But I live in Taos, now, sir," the cowboy said.

"How much do you weigh? You are huge!"

"Two-hundred and eighty-three pounds!"

Lee was certain that this man was the largest white person he had ever seen, and he could barely see the top of his head as he looked ahead. His head and neck seemed to be the same size. All he could see was the middle part of his back.

He was wearing dirty overalls and cowboy boots. His arms and neck were hot pink and his white, shaved, head looked funny in contrast to the rest of his skin.

Lee was next.

"Okay, what size are you, son?" the man asked.

Lee said nothing.

"Are you deaf, son? Not a big talker eh? Neely, get over here."

A small man with what looked like a thin strip of leather with numbers on it came up to Lee and placed the strip around Lee's neck.

"Neck, 15." The small man said and he wrote the numbers on a little card.

"Waist, 29."

"Inseam, 34."

"Chest, 34."

"Shoe size, 10."

"Next." the man behind the table said.

Lee was moved again and, in a moment of some freedom, and feeling lonely, he quickly tried to relocate some of his pals. Scouring the courtyard, he found a small group of them in a small bit of shade close to the building, isolating themselves from everyone else.

Lee walked over to them and greeted them with a hand-shake.

"You guys okay?" Lee asked.

"I have never seen so many white men in one place before," Curtis said.

"I knew they were white on the outside, but without their clothes on, they were even whiter," Walter laughed.

Curtis chimed in, "And they have too many hairs on their body; some of them look like bears!"

Lee smiled, "I am hungry. I need some fry bread."

"Stop thinking about that. I would die for some fry bread right now," Walter said.

Before they could continue they heard a loud whistle and they all turned to see where the sound was coming from.

All eyes were on the center of the courtyard where three men in uniforms were standing tall. They were all wearing hats that reminded Lee of Shiprock rock on a flat brim. Their voices could be heard throughout the courtyard. One had a voice so piercing, he sounded like an animal. Everyone started to scatter at their command. They formed several lines consisting of ten men across and twenty deep. Everyone was tensely quiet, looking forward. The Navajo Men in line tried to understand all that was being said, but they all had a hard time listening to the loud slurred English. One man of the men in uniform yelled out, "All right, men, we are here to train you to be United States Marines and we are here to train you to kill Japanese. You will be the meanest Sons a Bitches the world has ever seen. We are here to make you boys into men and the best and toughest killing machines this man's army can make."

Lee listened as the men shouted, but he had a hard time keeping up with everything that was being said. Curtis was having the same problem, and he turned to Lee, "I guess we should just follow what the white guys do."

"Yeah, just follow them. I don't know," Walter added.

The men in uniform continued to instruct the group while Lee and his friends tried to pick out the words they could understand and fill in the rest, "You men will be on a train to Camp Pendleton where your Basic Training will begin. There you will be put through hell and if you survive, you will be shipped out to kill the Nips."

"Move OUT!"

The group all turned and began to file out by rows. Lee and his friends were on the last row and would be the last ones on the train. The men in uniform hurried the group along by making them jog to the train; they would yell an occasional word or two to keep the crowd moving. As they got on the train, Lee looked in awe at the massive metal machine sitting there, smoking. Neither Lee nor his buddies had ever seen a train up so close before. The huge cars they were about to board looked bigger than three hogans. The five stepped up the steps and into the car. The seats were set like they were in the bus, but they were bigger. They all grabbed a seat and looked out the windows. Everything was so new to them, they felt excitement as they heard the whistle blow.

Lee sat quietly in his thoughts. *Brother, what did you feel? Did you feel scared or excited? Did you know that I was thinking of you as you left? I know you will be with me on my journey.*

Curtis looked over at Lee. "I wonder what California is like?"

"I had a cousin who told me it was real different from Shiprock," Walter chimed in.

"He told me that they have strange trees there. They look almost like a tree with no branches. And he said the ocean was bigger than any lake we have at home."

Lee, still lost in his own thoughts, was becoming a little

more excited about the train ride and his new adventure. This was the first time he had been able to think since he left Red Rock and he enjoyed watching the scenery pass. If he ignored the sounds of the men talking around him, he could hear the sounds of the train. As night fell they all slept and when day came they were in a land unlike any they had seen before. There was an endless array of buildings and cars and white people. Lee was fascinated by the new world he had just entered. Even the clothes the people were wearing were strange and unfamiliar.

The train slowly entered Los Angeles, where the group was ordered off and onto a bus, which took them south to Camp Pendleton. The bus stopped, two hours later, and everyone was ordered off and the group was herded through the big doors of a building next to the bus. Everyone filed in but no one came out. Lee went through the doors and was met by a man who asked him for his card. Searching his pocket for the card that the small man with the long strip had given him, he handed it to the man. The man checked his card and handed him a pair of green pants, shirt, socks, dungarees, and black boots. Then he was ordered to go and change. Lee stood and admired his new clothes. He had never had so many new clothes on at the same time. In the yard were twice as many men as were in Gallup, and after looking around he found that there were very few Navajo.

Five men in uniform came onto the field and immediately started yelling at the men. Lee found himself in the front row and got the attention of the first sergeant. Everyone stood up straight and looked forward. As the man in front of him was yelling into his face, all Lee could see was the inside of the man's mouth. Lee had never heard so much shouting from men before.

He had nothing to say but, "Yes, Sir."

"I can't hear you, Marine!" the man yelled.

"Yes, Sir," Lee repeated a little louder.

"You will address me with, Yes sir, Drill Sergeant, sir," the man screamed in his face.

"Yes, sir, Drill Sergeant, sir," Lee repeated.

The Drill Sergeant stepped back to speak to the rest of the crowd.

"For the next eight weeks this is your home. For those that don't know, we are at war and the next eight weeks will prepare you for that war. This might be the most difficult time of your life but I can guarantee that what you learn may one day save your life. So listen up. My name is Sergeant William T. McNally. I will be seeing your ugly faces every minute of every day. I am your Drill Instructor and you will follow every order I give you and if not I will kick your asses until you understand that I am God."

Lee looked forward, listening.

"When I dismiss you, you will be led to your barracks. You will need to find a bunk and then you will be taken to mess for chow. After mess, you will head back to the barracks and we will hit it hard in the morning. Fall out!"

The crowd was led line by line into the barracks.

As the group entered the doors, they quickly scattered to a bed. The beds were stacked one on top of the other and men were rushing past Lee.

I don't know why they are all running. They all look the same to me, Lee thought.

Each bed contained a blanket, two sheets, and a small pillow. The room smelled clean but different and as Lee looked around he tried to find an empty bed. It looked as if all the beds were taken. But then Lee spotted a bunk near the end of the room. A skinny white boy with red hair was setting up his bed on the top bunk and the lower bunk appeared to be empty.

"You can sleep down here. I don't think anyone is sleeping here," the red-headed boy said sheepishly.

Lee extended his hand and shook the boy's hand.

"My name is Phil Wheatly. I am from Wisconsin," Phil said.

"I am Lee Benally. I am from Red Rock, Arizona," Lee said.

"It's nice to meet you, Lee," Phil replied.

Lee felt good to have met a new friend and the two of them walked to the mess hall together. In the mess hall, there was more food than Lee had ever seen before. He knew he was hungry, but he couldn't imagine eating all the food that was placed before him. Even at home his mother would never have had that much food to give him for one meal. In fact, his tray contained enough food for his whole family. After dinner he and Phil headed back to the barracks.

As Lee lay on his bed he couldn't help but think of his home. *What is father doing? I hope mother isn't worrying about me. Have I done the right thing?*

One by one the men drifted off to sleep and the room became quiet. Lee drifted off to sleep as he looked up at the wires of the bed above.

It seemed as if he had just fallen asleep when he was awakened by a loud bang.

The Drill Sergeant's cronies were banging on a metal trash can with a stick. The noise in the room resonated until everyone was awakened.

"It's 4:00 in the morning," Phil said, surprised.

"Up and at 'em. We have a fun-filled day planned for you boys today," the Drill Sergeant shouted.

The men began rolling out of bed, groaning and moaning. Lee jumped up and felt rested and ready to greet the sun. Back home he would be up to get to the sheep, so he felt eager to start his day.

He quickly got on his clothes and stood at the foot of the

bed. Most of the others around were still struggling to get out of bed.

"It's too early," someone complained.

"What the heck? It's four in the morning," someone else groaned.

The Drill Sergeant began to yell at the staggering men to motivate them, and when everyone was standing, the Drill Sergeant herded the group outside. The Men shuffled into the courtyard, and were formed into two lines.

"Okay, girls, it's time to run. We will be doing five miles. You will not stop and you will not give up. Now let's go," the Drill Sergeant barked.

Lee was excited to get out and run. Running for him was something he had done everyday, and five miles was nothing. He was going to enjoy it. The sky was still dark and there was a cool wet breeze blowing off the ocean. Lee's pace seemed unstressed and he felt undeterred. A quarter of his bunkmates were complaining of thirst, headache, and cramps after the first hour. Some were even vomiting. Lee enjoyed seeing the new sights around him and he soon found himself at the head of the group. Many new sights caught his attention and he pondered the strange surroundings. Palm trees, ocean, and the sky all looked so foreign. The sky was beginning to show signs of the sunrise and Lee was ready to greet the day.

As he rounded the final curve up the last hill before he hit the barracks, Lee realized that only he, his Drill Sergeant, three other Navajo men and two skinny white boys were grouped together for the home stretch. Lee was tired but not exhausted. But he was confused at the purpose of running for no reason. There was always a purpose to run, to find sheep, or to run errands for father. . . *What is the reason for this?*

The other men came behind him, heaving and sick.

"Break for chow," the Sergeant yelled.

The mess hall was alive with activity.

I have never seen so much food, Lee thought, grateful for the meal after a nice run. *This is not what mother would prepare for us, but it tastes real good.*

Lee could hear others in the group complain about the awful food set in front of them. But it was all good to him.

After breakfast they were broken up into different groups for rifle drills. And so it went all day long.

At the end of the day, everyone was exhausted and ready for bed. After dinner and an evening run, they were dismissed to the barracks to sleep.

This rigorous activity continued for eight weeks.

As graduation came, Lee was awarded a medal for Marksmanship. He had done a lot of shooting of prairie dogs near his house and he was the best in his class. All of his other bunkmates were assigned to the South Pacific. But Lee had been asked to stay behind for a special Communications School.

As Lee reported to class at Camp Elliot, he recognized a handful of his friends from Shiprock and the surrounding areas. He found a seat and sat down.

"We have a special project for you soldiers that has proven successful for the last two years in combat," the instructor at the front of the class began.

"You will all be a part of a special operation that will be using a unique code that will involve your native language of Navajo."

I wonder why our language is important now. Special operations sounds important but it seems funny that now they want us to speak our language.

Lee found it interesting and was very willing to listen to the instructor.

"During the next four weeks you will study Morse Code,

Semaphore Signals, military message-writing, wire laying, pole climbing, communication procedures, and how to work radios. We will teach you how use this equipment and how to assemble and disassemble them in your sleep."

The instructor then cues a Navajo that it is his turn. The Man walked to the front of the room and stood in front of the class.

"My name is Sam Begay. I am from Pinon, Arizona. My mother is from the *Tseikeehe* (Two-Rocks-Sit) Clan, and my father is from the *Shash Dine* (Bear People) Clan. I know that all of you are craving some fry bread and mutton stew, but first we have a job to do. My job is to teach you 'The Code'. Only a few know about this code. Washingdon wants us to keep it secret. It is our job to teach you how to use this code in combat and we are the only ones who will understand it. Which one of you cannot speak or understand English very well? It is important to tell the truth because you need to be able to speak English," Sam instructed.

Two of the twenty men raised their hands.

"*Ha at'ii?* (What?)" Sam said pointing to the first man.

"At Fort Wingate at the Boarding School we were told not to speak Navajo. What if the Bilagaana change their mind and we get in trouble?"

"Yeah, and I was caught talking Navajo and I was sent underneath the school for two days. That was only five months ago. After that I didn't speak Navajo,"

Sam asked. "*What are your names?*"

"They call me David Attcity."

"My name is Ronald Todachinii."

The instructor was familiar with their concerns. He had seen the same questions from some of the previous "Code Talkers." He continued, "You all need to believe me. As your brother, I am asking you to trust me."

Almost immediately the entire class showed a look of

approval for their brother standing in front of them. And Sam, in turn felt their trust. Sam turned to the Bilagaana Instructor and the white man walked back to the front of the room.

"Okay, soldiers, we are going to start first thing in the morning. At 04:00 we will begin with some light running and at 07:00 we will start class. For you fellows that don't speak English very well, we need you to stay behind. The rest of you, unpack and head for chow."

Lee noticed that five of them stayed behind. Either they didn't speak or they had more questions. He headed to the barracks for some R and R. The barracks contained the same beds that he saw at basic training, but this time all of his bunk-mates were Navajo, not white.

It is going to be different not having to smell my white bunkmates.

Someone tapped Lee on the shoulder, and he quickly turned around. It took a moment for Lee to recognize the skinny, bald Indian, but after closer inspection he realized it was Thomas Tsosie.

"Lee!" Thomas said.

"What are you doing here? When I talked to your mother a couple of months ago, she told me that you were at Fort Wingate Boarding School," Lee said. "Does your mother know you joined the Marines?"

"I wrote to her on a postcard. I am hoping that someone at the trading post in Sanostee will tell her that I joined."

"Are you old enough?"

"Don't say anything. I think I'm fifteen years old but when the recruiter asked me if I was eighteen I just said yes. I just said 'Yes Sir' to all of his questions and they let me join and now I'm here." He paused. "I thought you and your brother were going to be medicine men like your father? Did your brother join too?"

"Yes, he joined too. About two years ago."

"Really? Has he told you about how it is out there?"

Lee slowly turned and tried to unpack. "He was killed."

Everyone that stood close to Lee and Thomas overheard Lee, and everyone was silent.

Navajo etiquette dictated that the dead should not be spoken of or talked about and Thomas quickly changed the subject. Pointing to the beds, he said, "You take the bottom and I'll take the top."

Thomas announced to the group, "Lee is a Medicine Man."

Everyone was excited and started to walk over to greet him.

Lee stopped them, "I am not a Medicine Man yet; I am still in training. My father is a Medicine Man."

The Men seemed relieved to have a holy man in their midst. One of the men approached Lee after the others dispersed. He asked quietly, "Will you do a ceremony for me? I have been having bad dreams that keep coming back."

"I'll see what I can do. Come see me later."

The young soldier extended his hand and shook Lee's hand in appreciation.

The Navajo departed with a calm sense of relief and hope. Lee returned to his unpacking and Thomas, who had jumped on the top bunk to lie down, leaned over and looked down at Lee and asked, "Do you shave?"

He didn't respond. Thomas grabbed a box of razors, held them up and yelled out, "Does anybody want my razors?" If he had offered his razors in any other barracks, he would have been able to give them to any white man in the group. But his offer fell on deaf ears. None of the Navajo shaved.

"I'll just keep these in case anyone needs them," Thomas said as he jumped off the bed and turned to Lee. "This is better than boarding school, isn't it?"

"I don't know, I have never stayed in a boarding school before."

"This is almost like boarding school but I think it's better."

"Why do you think it's better?"

"I get to run early in the morning, I get to have really good food, I get to shoot guns, I get to yell as loud as I want sometimes, and I now I even get to talk Navajo. The only thing missing is fry bread." As soon as Thomas finished his statement, the men in the barracks cheered.

One of the men standing next to the door said, "I think it's time to eat. Let's go."

Seven o'clock the next morning found all of the Navajo men in class. The blackboard in the front of the classroom had several rows of Navajo and English words written on it. Everyone who entered eyed the blackboard and wondered what was in store. When they were all seated, Sam Begay stood at the head of the classroom with a long stick in his hand. He pointed to the English word, COW. "David, what does this say?"

David answered, "It said Cow."

Sam then pointed to the Navajo word. "What is this word?" There was silence.

Sam spoke, "That is *Beegashii*. (Cow). It is very important that you know English because you will have to memorize over two hundred words in English and Navajo. The reason why is because you will need to know what the words for a battleship, destroyer, infantry, tanks, and aircraft are. You will need to know how to say them in Navajo and exactly what they mean in English."

Sam brought in another Navajo to demonstrate how fast 'The Code' was and how accurate they had to be.

"Na ats'oosi Wolachi Gah Hatin Bichiih Jaa Tl'iish."

It took Sam less that ten seconds to say those words, and it took almost fifteen seconds for George Nez to decipher and translate the words. Sam looked out at his class. "Does anyone know what just happened? How many know what I just said?"

Everyone in the room raised their hands.

"Okay, what was the first word I said?"

"Not the Navajo, the English word."

He pointed at Timothy Benally in the front row.

Timothy spoke up with confidence, "Mouse!"

Sam wrote the word MOUSE on the board.

"Very good. Who knows the second word?"

Someone yelled, "Ant."

Sam wrote the word ANT on the board directly under the first word.

Then most of the class said, "Rabbit."

"Ice."

"Nose."

"Ear."

"Snake."

As Sam wrote the English words on the board, it looked like

MOUSE

ANT

RABBIT

ICE

NOSE

EAR

SNAKE

Next Sam circled the first letter of each word and then asked, "Now what does this say?"

The entire class yelled out, "Marines!"

"Exactly. Now that was easy. For the next four weeks we will work on your speed and accuracy. The most important part of 'The Code' is accuracy. If you don't translate correctly, soldiers will die. It is very important that you understand that. We will spend eight hours a day learning this code and another four hours of learning the equipment for the next two weeks. The last two weeks we will spend eight hours on the equipment and fours hours on 'The Code' in combat exercises."

Four weeks later everyone received their new orders. Sam handed out the orders to the class.

"Where are you going?" Thomas asked.

"The Soloman Islands." Lee replied.

"I will be in Hawaii." Thomas smiled.

"I hope to see you again. Maybe I will come to your house when we get home and your mother can make us some fry bread and mutton," Lee replied.

Thomas extended his hand, "I will miss you. Make sure you be careful."

Lee shook his hand. "You be careful too."

Lee boarded the bus that took him to San Diego and from there he would board a ship bound for the South Pacific.

9

As Lee boarded the ship that would take him into battle, he was introduced to his new companion.

"I am Lieutenant Charles Murphy."

"My name is Lee Benally," Lee said extending his hand.

Lieutenant Murphy shook Lee's outstretched hand.

"Lee Benny?" he asked.

"No, Benally," Lee corrected.

"Well Benny, I guess we are going to be stuck together for a while," Murphy said.

Lee smiled and didn't argue.

Later that evening Lee had time to enjoy the open sea. He enjoyed watching the dolphins jump in front of the ship's bow. Inside the boat, everyone was packed in like sardines. There was no room to think and everything swayed if you wanted it to or not. Lee just tried to sleep. Everyone was quiet as if they might be praying. Everyone found God right before battle.

He was left with his thoughts and often questioned his mission.

What is my fate?

After a few weeks of sea travel, everyone got sick of the ocean. A soldier vomiting was a common occurrence. They had finally reached the Soloman Islands and in the morning they were near the shores of Bougainville. It was January and it should have been cold, but it was hot and the air was wet. As Lee entered the LST, his thoughts are of his brother. *Did he have to go through this?*

All that could be heard was the roar of the engines and all

that could be seen were all the helmets in front of him. As the boat landed and the ramp fell with a splash into the water, Lee was hit with the overwhelming smell of blood. Several high-pitched sounds flew toward the boat and exploded in the water sending a spray over the group as bullets pierced the helmets of the men on the front row. The men fell immediately to the floor of the LST and Lieutenant Murphy had to push Lee forward over his fallen friends so that he wouldn't be hit.

"Sorry Mack, we gotta get outta here," Lieutenant Murphy said, holding Lee down.

Lee looked to see if he could see the enemy, but all that could be seen were deadly flashes of light from the machine gun fire that was raining down on the whole beach. Lieutenant Murphy realized that the only way out of the LST was over the side so he grabbed Lee and they jumped into the water.

The sky was gray and the ocean below was red with blood.

For a brief moment there was a muffled quiet sound and Lee had a hard time seeing anything. But as he reached the surface, he took a big gulp of the salty seawater. The taste was strong and he quickly tried to spit it out, but the tide was high, and when another wave came in, he was hit with another dose.

It was hard for Lee to get his feet under him, primarily because of the hundred pound pack he was carrying, but he stood and found Murphy next to him.

Murphy, out of breath asked, "Where's your radio?"

Lee didn't say anything, but instead just pointed to the water.

"Okay, Mack, we need to find you a good working radio."

Lee and Murphy ran quickly over the bodies lying in the water. Lee had been told about the necessity of stepping over people, dead or alive. Navajo tradition dictated that it was taboo to step over someone lying on the ground, but Lee found it an easy tradition to disregard as they were trying to find cover. The men were running around trying to find cover. Lee tried to determine where the enemy was. All he could see were flashes of gunfire coming from the mountain—no faces.

Amid the unbelievable chaos, Lee and Murphy finally arrived on the beachhead.

The beach was covered with anti-tank barricades and barbed wire. The sound of yelling and screaming was almost unbearable. Lee had only a few seconds to look around. The few soldiers he got to know at Basic were now gone, and although he was surrounded by men, he didn't seem to notice anybody around him. The only sounds he could hear were the buzzing of bullets flying by, and high pitched sounds as the bullets hit the anti-tank barricades, and the deep thud of other bullets as they hit Marines.

"This is company A, first battalion sir. We're under heavy fire I thought this is going to be clean, but we're taking heavy casualties sir—over," the Sergeant screamed.

He and his Corporal were huddled under an anti-tank barricade and had a hard time hearing the radio communication.

"Say again, say again! Over."

There was an explosion. The water and muddy debris flew into the air. For a brief second Lee could feel a wave of heat on his face, and he was thrown back. He slowly got up through the haze of smoke. The Sergeant and the Corporal had all but disappeared and in their place was nothing but twisted metal and smoke.

Lee, without thinking, quickly started up the beachhead. He crawled toward a fallen Marine and picked up his M1 rifle.

Immediately in front of him was a group of Marines digging in for cover. They were shooting at the invisible enemy in front of them, but they were not sure if they were hitting anything at all.

"Hey Joe, I've been looking for you everywhere," Lieutenant Murphy said.

"My name is Lee Benally, not Joe," Lee replied.

"Sorry, Joe. You don't watch movies at all, do you?" Murphy replied as he quickly ducked down. Sand showered down on them after the huge explosion hit right in front of them.

"Movies? I don't know what they are, sir," Lee replied.

"Never mind, Private, let's find us a working radio," Murphy said holding up a radio box with several bullet holes in it.

Murphy was backed up against the makeshift barricade; the enemy was behind him. Lee turned to him and pointed down to what looked like a radio, almost a hundred yards away. If they could make it there, Lee could radio for help.

Murphy adjusted his helmet and wiped the sweat and dirt off his fore head. "Okay. . . ," he looked at Lee, "if we are going to do this we're going to do it now, come on soldier," Murphy said as he began to run in front of Lee.

There were sprays of bullets in front of them and the impact of the bullets on the sand shot up beach dirt into his eyes. Murphy quickly stopped just short of the radio. "I can't see, Joe," screamed Murphy as he put his hands over his face.

"It's going to be okay, sir," Lee said, "Hold onto my belt. I will get you over there."

"Yeah, that will work. Now don't get us killed, Joe? Hey, and when this is over we're going to watch a whole lot of movies, okay, pal?" Murphy said with worry in his tone.

"Yes sir," Lee replied, and they headed for the radio.

"You don't talk much, do you, Joe? Oh, I mean Benny," Murphy said.

"No sir," Lee replied.

"I know that your name is Benally but I think it sounds

better if I say Benny. I think it has a nice ring to it. Don't you?"

Lee quickly pulled Murphy down.

"We're here, sir," Lee said.

He took his canteen out and poured water into Murphy's eyes.

A medic ran and fell in the foxhole next to them.

"I'll help him out Private," the medic said.

"Okay Lieutenant, let me take look at this," he said as he reached into his medic bag and pulled out some ointment and bandages.

"I'll be Okay, Doc, it's just dirt," Murphy said.

"I know. But you'll need to keep your eyes covered for a few hours. You really scratched them up." He patted him on his helmet and quickly left to aid another.

"Benny, where are you?" Murphy asked. He was lying on his back feeling helpless.

He could only hear the endless noise of death and the familiar sound of a mobile radio being cranked up for use.

"There you go, Benny. Tell HQ that we need artillery fire on the north side of this beach head ASAP."

The next sound Murphy heard was a strange language coming from Lee's mouth. *I hope he is getting this or we're all going to die out here. Dear God, forgive me, I know that I should go to church. But I'm going to die out here.*

Murphy lay still as the message was sent.

"Benny, can you hear me, Marine? Hey Marine, I. . ." Murphy started.

"Sir, HQ said they are going to lay out fire here in five minutes, Sir," Lee said as he rested next to Murphy.

"Good job, Benny. Maybe we might live today," Murphy said as he leaned back.

"Yes, sir." Lee looked up in the sky. The sun couldn't be seen because the smoke was so thick.

I can't get this smell out of me, he thought. The smell of blood, machine gun fire, and many other smells he couldn't recognize, filled Lee's tense moment.

Brother, I can't believe you went through this. This is terrible. And the death...all the bad spirits around here. Father, please help me. I don't know if I can do this.

Suddenly, overhead, a rain of high-pitched sounds came down on the north side of the island. The explosions, as they hit, could be felt all up and down the beach.

"Yah hoo! Take that, Nips, see how you like that," screamed Murphy as he took off the bandage over his eyes and waved it like a flag above his head.

* * *

Victor stared at the pile of papers on the table. He carefully rifled through the pile and picked out his grandfather's tour schedule.

"Hey mom, look at this. It looks like grandpa's tour of duty. He served with the first, third, and fifth Marine division. Marshall Islands, Bougainville, Guam, and Iwo Jima," Victor said as they looked at the papers and his dog tags.

"Look didn't they get Grandpa's birthday wrong? It says he was twenty but he would have only been about eighteen," Victor concluded.

"Your Grandmother told me that there was really no way to know how old anyone was. So when the military asked them how old they were they would have to take the boys' word for it. He would have been around eighteen when he went," Betty replied.

The windows were open and Victor watched his boys playing outside.

A gust of wind blew through the window and scattered the papers onto the floor.

Victor was intrigued by the one of the papers left on the

table, and after closer inspection, Victor realized that it was an unfinished letter his Grandfather was writing to his friend.

As everyone tried to pick up the paper mess on the floor, Victor looked up briefly and saw a white owl outside the window. Victor walked slowly toward the owl and it was as if everything was moving in slow motion and everything else was drowned out. Victor looked at the owl and the owl stared back at him like he was communicating with him. As he got closer to the window he received a vision of his grandfather.

* * *

The air was cold and Victor and his grandfather were sitting down on the log outside the house. No one was speaking.

"Could you take a look at a letter that I started," Lee asked his grandson.

Victor was caught up in the excitement of his life and the new adventures ahead of him.

"Sure, I will help you. I can look at it tomorrow." Victor quickly answered his grandfather. Then he got back to his own thoughts, "My mission is going to be a short two years. It will be fun to be back here when I get back, we will have all the time in the world. I'll even bring by my new girlfriend."

Lee got a sudden chill as he heard the words of his grandson. "What did you say?"

"Huh?" Victor asked.

Lee was worried but did not let on to Victor that he had even the slightest concern.

"*Dao sa* (time to eat)," Mary called from the door.

Victor helped his Grandfather to his feet. "I'm sorry, what did you say?"

Lee waved his hand as if he were shooing a fly. "Something that you said reminded me of something. Something that someone said years ago."

* * *

Staring at the owl, Victor caught himself, shook his head slightly, and blinked rapidly. The owl turned quickly and flew away as a crackle of thunder could be heard rolling closer. The thunder rattled the room and Victor looked outside for the boys.

"Alec and Christian, hurry and come inside," Victor yelled.

The twins were playing out by the stack of wood and they acted as if they couldn't hear him until the thunder cracked again, this time closer. Alec and Christian stopped immediately, looked at each other, and then ran for the door.

Victor felt guilty and sad that he had let his grandfather down.

Should I be punished for this undoing? What is this owl telling me?

Victor saw Ray coming up the road in his oxidized Pontiac Sunfire with tinted windows. The car was Rez-ed out.

The wet breeze brought in the smell of wet pine and dirt. Which Victor really loved.

"Hey bro, finally rain!" Ray said as he put his arms in the air. He acted as if he had just scored a touchdown. He quickly grabbed a brown paper sack from the car and ran in for some shelter,

After everyone was safe in the house, Betty noticed her son. "Vic, you look like you saw something. Is there anything wrong? The last time I saw you look like that was the time we were walking in Sanostee, and we saw that lady."

"What Lady?" Allison asked.

"You don't want to hear this one, Allison." Victor said, hoping his mother would drop it.

Ray interrupted, "Oh, yeah. I haven't heard that story in a while." He grabbed a beer and quickly sat in his chair.

"It's not one of your Skin Walker stories is it?" Allison questioned. "Well is it or isn't it?"

"All my life I had always heard Skin Walker stories second hand", Victor said. "This is the first story that actually happened to me."

Though intrigued, Allison still didn't want to hear it. "It's going to bug me all night if you don't tell me, so just get it over with."

Victor wasn't the best storyteller, so he said, "I was just a kid at the time. You tell it better than I do, Mom."

Betty was willing to recall the story. She enjoyed story-telling. She sat down at the end of the table. The wind outside was pounding against the windows wanting to come in as she began. "Your Grandmother always wanted me to take her to the Revivals, so I had Phoebe and Darlene come with me. At midnight it was finally over. At that time the roads weren't paved and we were coming out of the boon docks, so it took us almost two hours to get back here to the house. Victor and his younger sisters were supposed to be asleep, but I guess Victor heard us coming in and woke up to see what we were up to. I guess he overheard that we were going into Farmington because I just got paid. But we needed to go to Sanostee first to get cleaned up and shower. His older sisters didn't want him to come along because he would just get in the way. That's what they said. But Grandmother changed their mind and told them they shouldn't treat their brother so bad. So now we had to take him along. Of course I wanted him to go, anyway," she said with a smile.

"So we headed out early that morning. As we were going, there was nothing wrong until we were only three miles from the house in Sanostee. We saw a vehicle on the side of the road by a sand dune and Phoebe slowed down to see if anybody was inside. I told her not to stop because if we did we would sink in the sand. She was a teenager, so of course she didn't listen so we got stuck. We tried for almost an hour but with no luck. So we decided that Victor and I should walk back to Sanostee to get some help. Victor and I started walking. But we didn't have a flashlight. I thought that was okay because the moon was full and there were no clouds." She shifted in her chair.

"We were only about a mile away from the house when Victor saw an old lady sitting next to the road. She was all dressed up in her traditional clothes. She had a yellow velvet skirt and a blue velvet blouse. She was sitting looking away from us and there was a dog next to her. I yelled at her to see if she was okay, but there was no answer. When we got about fifty yards from where she was, we were going to see if she needed some help. I started to talk to her in English and Navajo but still there was no answer. Victor kept pulling on my shirt. He kept wanting to go the other way. I finally cried out, "Can you hear me?" as we got closer. We came within ten feet and she finally turned her head and looked our way. Victor and I screamed and we started to run towards Sanostee. . ."

Pause.

Allison gripping her bottled water said, "So what happened?"

A gust of wind came through the old house and the lights went out.

There was a loud scream, but it wasn't Allison or Betty. It was Raymond.

Victor yelled, "Who was that?"

Raymond blurted out, "I think it was Allison. Are you okay?"

Betty got up, "It's okay." She shuffled over to the cupboard and found the Kerosene Lantern and put it in the middle of the table. "Raymond, that was you! I can't believe that a six foot three-hundred-fifty-pound Indian can scream like that." Betty said.

Ray, who was embarrassed by his reaction, said the first thing that came to his blurred senses: "I spilled my beer on myself and it's cold. You know how I get when I spill my beer."

Betty rolled her eyes and sat at the table.

"So what happened to the lady? Was she dead or something?" Allison asked.

"Yeah Allison, she was—something," Victor said.

Allison was puzzled by his response.

Betty jumped in, "Victor and I were only about ten feet away when she looked right at us. We got a good look at her face or what should have been her face. It was just black. . . hollow."

"You mean she didn't have a face? How can she not have a face, Victor? That's gross! You're kidding right?" Allison asked.

"Nope, that really happened. Scared the pants off me for years," Victor said.

Betty said, "The next day I was talking to one of our neighbors and they said that somebody had said the same thing."

As the story ended, Raymond stood up and pulled his chair closer to the table and smiled at everyone. Wanting to change the subject, he said, "So, did you see your white buddy again? You know the owl?"

Victor responded, "Yeah. It seems to follow me wherever I go."

The hiss of the Kerosene Lantern seemed to be the only sound in the room.

"If you see an owl during the day, it's a messenger. Grandpa used to tell us that," Ray said.

"Have you ever seen one?" Victor asked.

Ray looked almost disappointed and said, "No, I don't think so. My wife hit me so hard once that I saw little white birds for a while."

Victor, embarrassed about his cousin's comments asked, "How about you, Mom?"

"I have seen a number of them. Especially after your

Grandpa and Grandma died. I would see them all the time. I thought that they were following me and I thought they might be my parents looking in on me," Betty felt her emotions start to rise.

"Weren't you scared?" Ray asked.

"At first I was, but I felt that it was Grandpa and Grandma and it seemed to me that they were trying to tell me something. I ignored it for a long time and after a while it didn't bother me," Betty explained.

"You never told me that before," Victor said, surprised that his mother had never shared that with him.

"I've had the same feelings as well. I have had dreams about Grandpa for the last six months. And then I would see the white owl during the day after the dreams."

Allison interrupted, "You guys aren't supposed to be talking about this stuff, are you?" Allison was always a little freaked about stories she heard on the Rez and she didn't need to hear any more stories like the scary lady in Sanostee.

Everyone stopped talking and noticed the skies were darker. The rain started to hit the window and the top of the roof. The bucket in the corner of the room where the ceiling leaked, started to fill.

Ray's eyes were as big as belt buckles. "Yeah, we shouldn't be talking about this stuff. Yeah, you should stop."

Victor disagreed, "We have to talk about this because I think this all means something. I think that Grandpa wants to say something. And we have been ignoring him. It could be something, but maybe not. He wants us to do something. I have always felt that what Grandpa told me about dying is that we need to die as we live in peace and harmony. I wonder if Grandpa died without that peace and harmony? I wonder if I can help him? I think the life Grandpa lived as a youth is some-thing he never wanted us to live. I don't think he wanted to go.

And he never wanted to talk about it."

"Yeah he told me not to join the Navy. He told me to stay in school," Ray agreed. "I think we should help him," he concluded.

"I don't have any answers, and I'm not even sure what I am looking for, but I feel I need to help him," Victor said.

"Everything else got blown off the table except this. Lets find out what we can find with it," Victor started. He picked up the paper and looked at it carefully. *It's a letter and it is unfinished.*

To my friend Murphy 1953

I miss talking to you. Thank you for saving my life. It is hot in red rock, I am medicine man now.
Just wanted to tell you how beautiful it is here being so far away.
I do hope you forgive me for not writing and I hope things are well with you.

Victor put down the letter. "The last part of this letter sounds so familiar. I think that Grandpa tried to finish this letter with some of my letters that I wrote him while I was on my Mission. Betty, do you have some of the letters that I wrote?"

Victor felt sad and he let the letter fall to the table.

Ray, seeing his cousin's pain asked, "Do you want a beer? When I start feeling bad I just have a beer to make me feel better."

"No, but I could use a Coke," Victor said.

"I'll get one out of the truck," Allison said.

Victor could feel a headache coming on.

"Grandpa Lee could speak English but it was hard for him

to write down his true feelings. Speaking and writing English are two different things," Betty said. "Does anyone know who Murphy is?"

"I'm sure there has to be something in these papers about him," Victor hoped.

"Do you think Murphy is a girl?" Ray asked.

Victor wanted to say something but held back and just smiled.

"No, Ray. Murphy is not a girl," Betty disciplined.

Allison came in from outside only to hear the last comment and asked, "What girl?" She sat the Coke on the table next to Victor and handed him two aspirin.

Ray excitedly reported, "Grandpa had a girlfriend. He was trying to write a letter to her and it sounded real good."

"I don't know. I don't think so," Victor said, trying to concentrate.

"Do you really think Grandpa had a girlfriend?" Allison asked.

"Do you think she was really pretty? Maybe she was Japanese," Ray said.

"I don't think that Murphy was a girl. I don't know of any girls named Murphy," Victor said, getting annoyed.

"Murphy Brown. You know that chick on TV," Ray leaned back on his chair and clasped his fingers behind his head. "I bet it was a girl, huh, Betty?"

Victor didn't know what to think, but he knew his goofy cousin was not helping.

Ray wasn't helping look through the papers. He just sat in his chair looking up at the ceiling. "Maybe she was real tall. She could have been short but I'm sure she wasn't fat."

Victor looked at Ray and gritted his teeth. He wanted to say something, but he stopped himself. "I think you need another beer."

Ray took that as an invitation and got up to open the fridge. "Any other takers?" He looked around the room and saw that no one took him up on his offer.

"How about you Allison? Do you want a cold one?"

"No, Ray," Allison said.

He snapped his fingers and said, "All right, no takers."

He took his can and walked toward the door. "I'll be back in a flash."

Victor was relieved for a moment that he could look through the papers without the noise. He found an old picture and looked closely at it. The picture contained Lee and a white man standing in front of an army jeep. There were palm trees in the background and the White Man had his arm resting on Lee's shoulder. Victor turned over the picture and discovered a name, address, and a brief inscription.

Charles Murphy

124 Cambridge Avenue

Boston, Mass

To my pal, Benny. Drop me a line when you get back to the states.

"I wish he would have talked to me about writing that letter. I don't write that well but I could have helped him. He was always too proud to ask for help," Betty said.

"I would think that being a Code Talker that he had to be able to speak and write English," Victor said.

"Wouldn't that have been military vocabulary? Vic, on your mission you were able to speak and understand German, but if you would have been asked to write down your feelings you may have had a hard time expressing yourself," Allison said.

Raymond quietly reentered the room.

"I know what you mean. I tried to write my wife that I would be back next week but I couldn't write that good so I just wrote 'see you later.' She got real mad," Ray said smiling.

"Thanks Ray. That helps," Victor said, sorry that his cousin was back.

Betty studied a piece of paper, "Look over here. He entered the military the summer of 1943 and he was in camp Pendleton for eight weeks. It looks like his first tour was in the Soloman Islands for six months."

"In 1945 it looks like he was in Iwo Jima. When the war was over he spent some time in Guam and then he came home. Here are his discharge papers." Victor set everything down and was ready to say something but was unsure of the right words. "Why? I don't understand this whole thing. I don't understand what the whole secret was. I don't understand the reason for all of this."

Betty tried to reason, "I don't know why he did that. All I know is what Grandpa told me. In my discussions with your Grandma I learned that he never got over the death of his brother. He was depressed for years after he vowed that he would never talk about or reveal his role in what he did. I don't have the answers you are looking for. I am just telling you what was told to me. I am not as intellectual as you are. Your Grandpa thought that you had the intelligence to think like a Medicine Man and you would be the only one who would understand him. He was so proud of your life and the decisions that you had made even though you didn't become a medicine man," she paused, then continued.

"Your travels to other countries made you a messenger of peace, while his job was to kill. For a medicine man, taking a life goes against everything he stood for. Grandma said that the reasons why he wanted to go were anger and revenge. It was against your Great Grandpa's wishes. No, your grandfather didn't want to draw attention to himself. He did it to help people. He became a very good Medicine Man. He wanted to have children. At the end of his life he did share some of his life with someone. He shared the best with all of you. I really don't think he wanted everybody to make a big deal about this part of his life."

"Okay, what am I supposed to do? We have learned about his life but what now? Since we're just beginning to know about this, let's see where it will take us," Victor said.

Betty recalled, "There is something interesting that your grandma told me while we were planting corn. You were away at college. She said that Grandpa always said that it was important to live each day of your life like it was your last. She said that Grandpa would always remember everyone he came in contact with. He always appreciated the grandkids who visited him. For him that was one of the most important things. I don't think that your grandpa meant to hold anything back or hurt you. You were important to him like all of his grandkids, but he felt you had the spirit of a medicine man. Whatever he is trying to tell you, is between you and him. You are close enough to him and your spirits are so much alike that you will figure it out."

The storm outside was beginning to end and the sun was trying to shine through the clouds. The sand had turned to mud and a small stream of water was running just outside the door.

Ray walked over to open the windows.

Victor chuckled, "All of this stuff is giving me a headache. I just wish he would have told me."

Betty picked up the shoebox that contained the letters addressed to Grandpa. "Let's look at this," she said.

"Pick a letter out of the box and see what it says," Victor said.

"This one has a return address from Massachusetts and the post mark is 1972," Allison said. She carefully opened the envelope and removed the letter.

"Here honey, you read this," Allison said as she handed the letter to Victor.

"Hey, Victor, read it out loud but don't read it too fast," Ray ordered.

Victor cleared his throat.

Dear Benny,

I am hoping that you have been receiving my correspondence. I hope that everything is all right with you. I continue to write these letters because I find that it is very therapeutic for me. I think I may have told you before but I have two sons. Nathan is the oldest. He is twenty-six. And Benjamin—we call him Benny—is twenty-three. I named Benny after you. My wife and I are anxiously awaiting the arrival of our first grandchild. Nathan's wife is due around Christmas.

I got to thinking about you and our time in Hell together. I hate bringing up the past memories but the only thing good about the war was my friendship with you. The reason why I am writing you now is because of your philosophy of life. I miss our conversations and I think about our time together daily. I really appreciated your insights of your native culture. I wish so much to meet up with you again. I want my family to meet you—I talk about you to them often. Remember the time we were waiting for the Japs in Bougainville before we had captured the island. . .

Lieutenant Murphy stepped out of protocol and sat down by Benny in the Battleship Mess hall. "Hey, Private, we have been together for a whole year and I still don't know a lot about your family. You are not much of a talker except around your pals. I would like to start to get to know you a little better."

Lee just looked at Murphy, not sure what he should say.

"I just got a letter from my gal. We are going to get married after the war. Do you have a girl, Benny?" Murphy said as he handed him a picture of Angela.

She is really white, thought Lee, but he said, "She is pretty," and handed it back.

Murphy took the picture, kissed it and put it back in his pocket, "I just got this great letter from her," Murphy said excitedly.

Lee started to say something but. . .

"Oh, I'm sorry. Were you going to say something?" Murphy asked.

"No, that's Okay," Lee said. *I'd like to tell him about Mary at Wheatfield Lake but I'd better not say anything I will just listen to him.*

"Angela is in College. She wants to be a nurse and she says she wants to be an army nurse. But I don't want her to see all of this war," Murphy said.

Lee listened to the story as if he hadn't heard it all before, though he had.

An alarm sounded and everyone was ordered to their quarters.

The men hurried to eat what they could on their plates and Lee and Murphy look at each other as if to say, 'here we go.'

Back in the barracks, Lee met up with his Navajo friends and they all exchanged small talk. Lee received a handshake of "Good Luck" from all of his friends and then headed to board the LST.

The first wave of landing craft headed onto shore and Murphy was amazed at the ships and the men storming the beach.

"Do you have all your equipment Benny?" Murphy asked.

"Yes," Lee replied.

"Make sure your radio works," Murphy advised.

"Yes sir everything works fine," he said.

"Do you have the orders?" Murphy asked.

"As soon as we hit the beach I am to radio division head-quarters," Lee said.

The doors opened and the Marines that had arrived just before them were held up on the beach.

"Follow me. We have to set up a place for communications over there," Murphy said, and pointed to an empty piece of beach.

Mortar fire followed them all the way to their cover and they rest near a small company of men.

All they could see was the fire from the machine guns, but no faces.

Lee cranked up his radio. "Trapped, we need artillery fire."

"How long have you been here, Sergeant?" Murphy asked the man next to him.

"About two hours," the Sergeant said. "No one is moving. They can't get a strong hold."

The sun was setting and night was almost upon them.

Lee called in the communication and stopped to watch the Sergeant unexpectedly scramble up the embankment and run. Murphy and Lee looked at each other, confused. Gunfire could be heard. Then after it quieted, a man could be heard calling for help.

Lee wanted to help, but with the dim light of dusk it was hard to see too much of anything.

He knew he needed to help, or the Sergeant would die.

Almost without thinking, Lee jumped out of the foxhole to the aid of the wounded man.

"Come back here!" Murphy yelled, "That's an order."

Murphy watched helplessly as the man he was ordered to protect, ran away from him.

Don't do that! I don't want you to be killed, he thought.

He watched as Lee reached the wounded Sergeant and knelt down beside him.

Just beyond Lee, he could see seven Japanese soldiers making their way down a small hill and if something didn't happen quickly, the enemy would stumble on Lee and the Sergeant.

Murphy was the only one with the ability to do anything. Yet all he could do was to sit motionless and paralyzed.

Do I try to shoot the Japanese? No, there are seven of them. I can't kill them all. But, what about Benny?

* * *

"Lieutenant Murphy, your mission is to keep your Code talker alive at all costs. But if he falls into enemy hands the Code could be compromised. Your mission is to protect him if you can, but you are under direct order to shoot your Code Talker in the event he may become captured by the enemy. Do you understand Lieutenant?"

"Yes Sir!"

* * *

Benny, NO! I can't.

Murphy felt the only help he could give his friend, was to honor the integrity of the Code.

As the sweat and tears fell from his face, Murphy put Lee in his cross hairs. As he was ready to fire, he noticed his arms and fingers were shaking. His beating heart and sweaty palms made the next ten seconds seem like hours.

The enemy was fast approaching and as they came down, they spotted Lee.

Now Murphy was out of time.

God, Help me. Murphy pleaded as he squeezed the trigger to end the life a man whom he had grown to care for and respect.

He fired. *I killed him*, he thought in horror as he looked to find no sign of Lee and he emptied his clip in anger on the Japanese soldiers.

Murphy quickly grabbed another clip and was about ready to shoot but realized that there was also a barrage of gunfire coming from Lee's last position.

Lee yelled, "Don't shoot, we got them!"

Murphy yelled in disbelief, "Is that you, Benny?"

"Yes, sir," Lee said, beginning to make his way out of the small ravine carrying the Sergeant over his back.

"Medic," Lee yelled, out of breath. He carried the Sergeant over his shoulder. The Sergeant had sustained gunshot wounds to his leg and abdomen and needed immediate attention.

Murphy was so overjoyed he almost jumped out of the foxhole. "Don't you ever do that to me again," he said grabbing Lee's shoulder.

"He would have died if I didn't do it," Lee said.

If you do that again I will have to kill you, but I can't tell you that, Murphy thought.

"Just be careful and just don't leave me like that again. Just stay alive," Murphy got up and walked away for a moment.

By dawn the beachfront had been secured.

Murphy had slept very little that night and needed to stretch.

"Where are you going?" Lee asked.

"I just need a minute."

"Don't go. You could get hurt."

"Gee, Benny, when I get back we'll have all the time in the world. Hey, maybe I can tell you more about my gal. She's a real dame!"

Almost as soon as Murphy left, Lee heard three shell explosions behind him.

He jumped out of the foxhole to find that Murphy had been wounded. Lee pulled him back into cover and realized the severity of his wounds.

"Medic! Medic! Medic!" Lee yelled and turned his attention

back to his friend. He tried not to alert Murphy of his wounded leg, which was half gone.

"It will be okay. You're going to be fine," Lee said.

Murphy's glassy and hurt eyes closed and Lee's first fears were that his friend was dead.

The Medic reached Murphy and took some quick Vitals.

"He has just fainted from shock," the Medic said as he started to treat Murphy's wounds. "Here hold this," he said, placing Lee's hand on a thick bandage packed over what was left of Murphy's leg.

Lee put pressure on the wound and softly chanted a prayer to help his friend.

He stood on the beach watching Murphy travel back to the ship and for the first time during his entire tour, he was alone.

I just wanted to write to you and thank you for saving my life. I wanted to tell you that I'm sorry. I have wanted to tell you this for many years, but I have not been able to. I was ordered to take your life and I am haunted that I had to keep that from you. I hope these letters are getting to you. I will never forget you.

Your friend
Charles Murphy
P.S. Please write to me or call me. God bless.

"This White guy was going to shoot Grandpa?" Ray asked.

"That's what it sounds like. It also sounds like he is sorry for all of that," Victor said.

"Wow," Betty replied.

"Hey, here's a letter from Hawaii. It is from Murphy," Allison said handing the envelope to Victor.

Victor opened the envelope and removed the letter and a picture.

Dear Benny,

I am recovering in Hawaii. I will be heading back to the States in a few weeks.

Corporal Hansen who was in our Platoon told me that you did a swell job at Iwo Jima when you all went up and took the island. He told me. . .

10

February 19

"Lee, the Lieutenant is waiting for you inside." Hansen said

Lee said nothing. He stood on the deck of the destroyer and looked out on the sea, filled with battleships, frigates, and aircraft carriers.

He took the corn pollen out of the leather pouch his father had given him and sprinkled the fine particles through his fingers, letting it drop out of sight off the edge of the boat.

"What are you doing?" Hansen asked.

"There will be much death in the near future. I need to protect my spirit."

"I'm scared too, private."

Lee acknowledged him, "Let's go."

Lee and Corporal Hansen entered a small classroom-type setting where there were about twelve other Navajos and a handful of officers in the room. Lee recognized his friends from Code school. He had seen his Code buddies throughout the war in different battles. He gave them a half smile as he entered.

As Lee sat, he felt tension in the room. He felt the need to listen carefully to what was being said and it was apparent to everyone else in the room to do the same.

Colonel McConnell stood at the front of the group, looking at the men sitting in front of him. He glanced at his aid, who motioned that all the men had been accounted for, and nodded for the teacher to begin.

He shuffled the papers in front of him and cleared his

throat. He then turned to a map directly behind him

"We have been bombing this island for the last sixty-two days. We are now preparing to take it. The results of the survey told us that the best possible landing sites are here on the Southern-most end," he tapped the map with his pointer, disclosing the area.

"There are approximately 21,000 Nips that have dug deep into this island," he paused for a moment tapping the pointer in his palm.

"Men, we are going to embark on a mission that is one of the largest Marine forces that have ever been assembled. There are a lot of Marines out there who will be depending on accurate communication. This mission requires you men to be accurate and fast." he cleared his throat again.

The years of smoking made his voice deep and gruff. He habitually patted the pocket of his uniform to locate the packet of Lucky Strike Cigarettes, took one out of the box and placed it in his lips. He then found a match and lit it up. The smoke immediately seemed to fill the already-cramped quarters and he motioned for the Lieutenant who scurried across the room and handed a paper to the Colonel.

"I am going to read off the list of names. You and your company will be a part of the first attack tomorrow morning. Begay, Eddy; Begay, Harold; Benally, Paul; Benally, Franklin; Thomas, John; Johnson, Albert; Nakai, Edward; Nez, Thomas. You fellas stay close to your officers. The rest of you will report to the radio room at 06:00. Privates, you are dismissed," the Colonel waited for the room to clear of all the Navajo men. And he quickly motioned to his aid to shut the door behind the last one. He crushed his cigarette into an ashtray as the men looked on.

Clearing his throat again he said, "This operation is top secret. I want you to keep your Code Talkers alive at all costs.

If anyone gives you any trouble, have them report to me. There are only a handful of us that know about this program and I want it to be kept that way. Any violation of this order and you can count on a Court Martial." He stopped.

"This island is vital. You are under direct order to protect 'The Code.' You know the importance of this order and you may have heard this a hundred times; well I'm going to tell ya a hundred more times. If your 'Code Talker' is in danger of falling into enemy hands, you are ordered to eliminate him to preserve 'The Code' at all cost. Your orders are clear. Dismissed!"

"Yes, Sir!"

All of the officers cleared the room, leaving the Colonel and his aid behind.

The officers had said yes, but they looked as if they hoped they wouldn't have to resort to shooting anyone but the enemy.

11

05:30

Lee reported to the Radio Room. He had slept very little the night before and shook off the urge to yawn. The officer on deck began to address the orders of the day.

"We've been firing on this sector all night with our 16-inch guns from here and our B 24 bombers earlier this morning," he said while pointing to Mount Suribachi on the map that was on the table.

The men all gathered around.

"Our first wave is leaving in a few hours. There are two sets of Code Talkers. The first group is Nakai and Nez. They will be with Charlie Company. The second pair is is Benally and Begay. They will be with Abel Company. I want to make sure that all your radios are working, so let's get started on testing."

The officer motioned to the soldier nearest the coffee canister. "Hey, Mack why don't you pour me a cup of joe. While you're at it, pour these fine men a cup too."

The seaman started to pour the coffee.

"What to do think about this, Lee?" Begay asked.

"I don't know, but I think it's going to be a long day," Lee replied, sipping his cup of coffee.

010:30

"We still haven't heard from Abel Company yet, sir," Lee said.

"How long has it been since you've heard from them?" the officer questioned.

"It looks like a half an hour ago. That's just after we asked them for their position," Lee answered.

The officer was interrupted with new information.

"We have heavy casualties in that sector. It looks like those Nips are dug in deep. They're really putting the heat on those boys.

The officer nervously looked around, then asked, "What about the regular radio guys?"

"I tried them too, but still, no one answers. I called Charlie Company but they're too far away and they're under heavy fire also."

The officer quickly turned and picked up the receiver of a phone to make a call.

There was a moment of silence filled with the endless chatter of soldiers on the radio asking for help. The sky outside was full of smoke and the bright light of the countless guns and rockets firing from the ships' cannons.

The officer set the phone down and paused. He looked over to Lee and his group and motioned for him to come over. "Okay boys, it's your turn. I just got off the phone with the Colonel. We need to reopen the communication line with Abel Company. So the two of you need to saddle up and go. We don't have much time left. Get going. Dismissed."

The officer saluted and Lee and Yazzie hurried to gather their gear.

Within fifteen minutes, they were on a Landing Ship Tank headed for shore.

Everyone said very little as they approached the volcanic ash-blackened beach and the sounds of war began to get louder as they neared.

As they headed inland, there was a blanket of high-pitched shells above them.

The constant machine gun fire and mortar explosions seemed like they would never end. The LST (Landing Ship Tank hit the beach head.

"Okay, fellas, this is your stop," the driver screamed through the chaos of battle.

The men quickly exited and ran to the nearest foxhole for cover.

Lee turned to Yazzie. "I liked it better on the ship."

"You know this place kinda looks like Crownpoint without the white people and the Nips," Yazzie said.

"I thought you told me that you were from Sheep Springs? And what about the shooting around here?" Lee asked.

"I am from Sheep Springs, but my girlfriend lives out in Crownpoint and her mother doesn't like me. A couple of times she shot at me. So this is what it might look like if I married her," Yazzie said.,

Lieutenant Yates interrupted, "Listen up fellas this is the message we need to send: *Heavy fire from the base of the mountain. Three pill boxes pinning men down. We are sustaining heavy casualties. We need flame throwers, not gunfire. The men are too close.* You got that Private?"

"Yes, Sir," Lee answered.

Yazzie quickly cranked up the radio and began to relay the message. Only a couple minutes passed and the responding message was received.

"Reinforcement is on its way. They also ordered us to find the other two Code Talkers immediately," Lee said.

Lieutenant Yates looked over the embankment to see the layout and quickly ducked back down. He then looked over his squad and took off his helmet to wipe the sweat off his forehead. He cleared away some of the debris off the sand and drew a crude map with a stick. He made sure that everyone could see, and then said, "Okay fellas, we're right here, and Abel Company is suppose to be right here. But they're not. Jones and Carter, I want you two to head up the middle here. Tidwell and Bailey–hey, Bailey, listen up. I want you two to take a flanking position on the left side. We'll be following you.

Our tanks are coming in in a few moments. Does everybody understand?"

"Gee, Lieutenant Yates, you're a regular swell guy. We're going right into a meat grinder," Jones answered.

"Heya, Mack, I don't like it too much either, but it's an order."

"You and the Top Brass are a couple a fine pals to send us into this mess, first," Jones rebutted.

The Lieutenant ignored the comments and looked over to see if the tanks had arrived yet.

"Okay, here she comes. Jones, Carter, get ready to take off."

As the tank slowly neared their position, Jones and Carter stood at the ready.

"Let's go Mack, it's time to shove off," Jones yelled.

Carter picked up his M1 rifle and the two jumped across the small embankment.

The others watched but only for a moment.

"Tidwell, Bailey, its your turn. Hurry up fellas, we don't have all day."

The two quickly ran to their position.

"Okay, the resta of ya, let's go. Benally, Yazzie and myself will be picking up the rear. Now let's move it, boys," the Lieutenant shouted.

The rest of the Company slowly walked toward their objective and finally reached what was left of Abel Company. The dead bodies and wounded were lying as far as one could see. They could hear men yelling, and as they turned, they could see a small group of men on the other side of the ridge, waving their hands and shouting.

"Lieutenant, you think . . ." Hansen started to say, but was interrupted.

"Jones and Carter, go check it out. And watch your six, fellas."

They both nodded and took off toward the ridge.

A few minutes later they could be seen returning with a few men. They were all slowly coming down the ridge. As they came closer, the Lieutenant pulled aside one of the soldiers.

"What happened, private?"

"What, sir? I can't hear very well with the shelling," the private pointed to his ear.

"WHAT HAPPENED, PRIVATE!" the Lieutenant shouted.

"This morning our platoon got cut in half. All the officers are KIA and our radios are shot to heck, Sir," the weary soldier replied.

"How many of your platoon are left?" Lieutenant Yates questioned.

"WHAT?"

"Never mind," he said, patting the soldier on the shoulder, knowing that he probably didn't hear him. He pointed for him to sit down.

"There is still heavy fire coming from there. But where are the other Code Talkers?" the Lieutenant said.

One of the soldiers from the ridge overheard the Lieutenant. "Say Mack, are you looking for your Indian pals?"

"Yeah, have you seen them?" he anxiously replied.

"About an hour ago they were by that blown-out pillbox over there. Gee, I sure hope they got outta there in one piece."

"Me too. Jones, Tidwell the six of you take off and find them fast. If you don't find them within an hour I want you to come back," the Lieutenant ordered.

He motioned to the others, "You two stay here. We don't need you fellas missing too."

"What do think happened to them? I hope they didn't get killed," Yazzie said.

Lee didn't answer. He leaned over to see the other men rushing up the hill through heavy machine gun fire.

"I don't think that they are dead," Lee finally answered.

"How? Oh, I forgot, you're the Holyman," Yazzie looked at him and put a cigarette into his mouth.

"I wanted to be a medicine man but there were too many songs to memorize and the stories are too long. I guess I just like herding sheep." He then asked, "Why are you here?"

Lee's mind was somewhere else. Yazzie began to speak again. "My father is always mad about something and my mother is mean, too. Maybe I joined the Marines to get away ,but now everybody here is mad too. Everyone is shooting the Nips for this ugly place. I wonder why, but our job is to send messages. I guess it's not bad. What do you think, Lee?"

"I think that you do a really good job," Lee said.

His thoughts went back to his missing brothers and he concentrates his concern on them.

An hour and a half passed, and the Lieutenant was about to assemble another party to find the others.

"Lieutenant, we found them," yelled Jones.

Lee heard them yell, and quickly looked over the foxhole.

They watched as the team made their way toward the Company.

Lee recognized Benally and Begay as they followed behind. Covered in mud, they were almost unrecognizable. If he didn't know better, Lee would have assumed that they were a couple of Japanese soldiers.

"Lieutenant, Bailey and Mckenzie bought it. We were under attack by those Nips. They are all over the place. I can't believe that all that shelling from our side didn't even make a dent."

Frustrated and angry, Jones jumped in for cover.

" It looks like you guys took a fine beating. Can you tell me what happened?" Lieutenant Yates asked as he looked at the beaten soldiers.

"Well, at first we were okay, but then the Nips came from nowhere. There were maybe twenty of them. They came in from all sides. Benally and me tried to radio in, but they came in too fast. Our squad was taken out in just under a minute, I think. We were covered in the black sand and we were lying down like we were dead. The Nips looked right at us and left. It happened real fast. The last few hours we have been trying to fix our radio. It got shot up real good. Sir," the shaken private said.

"Boys, I'm glad you're all right. Have a seat. Benally, get ready to radio this into the skipper."

"Aye, sir," Lee answered.

Lee relayed the message and waited for a message to return.

"Message received. We need to stay here until we receive new orders, sir."

"Very well. Carry on, private. It looks like we can take a little break," the Lieutenant said.

"So what happened out there, Harold?" Lee questioned, setting his radio down.

"Nobody knew what was going on. The sergeant was the only one who had seen some action. They started to shoot from every direction so everybody took off. We were stuck with the Lieutenant, but he didn't know what to do. He was yelling at me to call for reinforcements, but we kept telling him that the radio was shot up. We couldn't fix it. Well, Paul started to yell at the Lieutenant to shut up. And the Lieutenant kept yelling back, "I don't understand you." We started to head back down when the big problem started. The Nips came up and they took the Lieutenant out. Me and Paul threw the radio away. It had been shot, and it had bullet holes in it. We both jumped into a small pond to hide, and when we got out we were all muddy. I think the Nips thought we were one of them. We just walked almost right by them. They looked right at us and they didn't say anything," Begay said, bewildered.

They all laughed.

12

Feb. 23, 1945

"It looks like Abel Company has heavy casualties they tell me seventy five percent," Lieutenant Yates said looking down at his report. "Sergeant Young, I want you to take your squad up Mount Suribachi. Then Lieutenant Schaffer will meet you half way. He and a couple of men are waiting for you."

"Right away, Sir," Sergeant Young answered.

Sergeant Young, took Lee and Private Yazzie with him up the hill and they were met half way by Lieutenant Schaffer.

"It's about time you fellas showed. Sergeant, do you have the flag ready?" Lieutenant Schaffer asked.

"I have it right here, Sir," Sergeant Young answered.

"Good, let's go."

The squad walked up to the top of the mountain without any enemy fire or confrontation.

"This view is amazing. You can see the whole island from here. Look over there you can see the whole fleet," Sergeant Young said.

"Okay boys, we need to find a pole or something to put this flag up," Lieutenant Schaffer said.

"Over here, Lieutenant," someone yelled.

"Great, you guys put up the flag. Benally, Yazzie and I will stay back to radio this in."

Lee cranked up the radio and relayed the message that the hill had been taken.

When they looked up, they saw the flag raised high on a long piece of pipe.

As Lee looked down at the fleet below, the ships horns began to blow and the cheers of the soldiers and seamen drowned out the sounds of war.

After securing the mountain, there was a small trickle of reporters and press wanting to capture the moment. They were all shuffling around asking questions and interviewing some of the men. Off to the side, some of the reporters were setting up Camera equipment.

"What are these guys up to?" Yazzie asked.

"They said they are going to put up another flag. I guess that one isn't big enough," Lee said as he noticed a handful of Marine and Army soldiers heading toward them.

One of the men walked toward Lee. Lee could tell that he was also an Indian.

Lee extended his hand, "*Ya'at'eeh.*"

The other man extended his hand and said, "No, I'm not Navajo."

"Where are you from?" Lee asked.

"Arizona."

"Me too. I'm from Red Rock."

Just as they began their conversation a reporter interrupted. "It looks like they are about to raise the flag. They could probably use your help."

Lee and the other Indian start to walk up toward the flag.

"Hey, Private!" a camera man, behind the two said.

"Could you hold this for me?" He handed Lee a bag and a camera.

Lee held the camera and watched as his new friend walked up and helped raise the flag.

13

Victor rose at 4:00 a.m. He walked the path that he and his Grandfather took to get to the lake. Quietly and thoughtfully, Victor sat down next to Grandpa and Grandma's gravesites.

As he overlooked the valley Victor's thoughts were of his Grandpa and the life he had just discovered.

Grandpa used to tell me about how he and his best friend would run up this hill. His best friend was his brother. And after all Grandpa saw and all he experienced, his heart and spirit were always here. And here is where he will stay. Forever.

The sun started showing itself on the horizon and Victor's attention turned to the eagle in the sky. Its shadows reflected off the Lake.

"It is important to know the past to appreciate the future. Life is something to be treasured and enjoyed," Victor could hear his grandfather say. "Good or bad, the past is what molds us and makes us what we are today. It is our choice to continue the path or not."

"It is my responsibility to carry on the stories for my boys," Victor said quietly.

He started back to the house with a renewed sense of purpose.

When Victor returned he began to finish the letter his Grandfather had started.

After the letter was finished, he drove down to the Trading Post and placed the letter in the outgoing mail.

Dear Mr. Murphy,

My name is Victor Bishop. I am the Grandson of Lee Benally and I have just recently discovered about my Grandfather and his involvement in the war. It might seem strange that I am just now learning of this part of his life but my Grandfather was very private and we have come to find out that his life in the war was something that he wanted to protect us from.

Grandfather passed away twelve years ago, but he very much wanted to write to you. Grandpa was a very private and proud man who was not one to ask for help. Unfortunately we were unable to hear his need for assistance in finishing this letter, but through certain events we have been able to piece together his wishes.

I can only speculate how he was feeling. It is apparent to me that he respected you and considered you a good friend. Knowing my grandfather was a man of peace, and had a love for life, I think that he would forgive you that day that you shot toward him as he saved the Sergeant.

It is my hope and the hope of my family that you understand how much he appreciated all the letters you sent to him. It sounded like you were both good friends and I think it is important for you to know that his spirit lives on and it was his wish that we keep his story alive.

May god bless you in your many endeavors.

Victor Bishop

Victor returned back to the house and waited for Allison and the boys to return from Shiprock.

Betty's truck could be heard outside the door and Victor, excited to see his family again, greeted them. The boys jumped out of the truck and ran to hug Victor.

"Daddy!" They yell in unison.

Victor bent down and scooped them up in his strong arms. The small bodies almost disappeared in Victor's embrace.

Victor then caught Allison's eye as she was closing the door of the truck.

She was smiling and as she came closer to hug Victor, she began to cry.

"What's wrong?" Victor asked as the boys slid out of his arms to the ground.

"Nothing sweetheart," Allison said.

"Did you go into Farmington? What happened?"

"Your mother took me into the Clinic in Shiprock," she said.

"Are you okay?" he asked.

"Yeah, nothing nine months won't cure," she said through her tears.

Victor grabbed Allison and hugged her tightly.

"Let's take the boys and go for a walk. Are you up to it?" Victor asked.

"Sure. Let me get their jackets."

Victor led his family up the trail to his grandparents' grave and he told the boys how his grandfather would walk with him on this same trail when he was their age.

"What's that?" Alec asked pointing to the grave marker.

"This is where your great grandfather and great grandmother are buried. Did you know that your great grandfather was a medicine man? And he had a twin brother just like you do. . ."

"Look at the white bird," Christian said, looking up in the sky.

Victor smiled, "That's an owl, son."

"Where is he going?" Alec asked.

"Home."

About the Author

Dory J. Peters

    Dory J. Peters resides in North Ogden, Utah with his wife and three children.

    Dory is the CEO and President of First Manhattan Funding, LLC in Ogden, Utah. He can be reached by e-mail at **dorypeters2002@yahoo.com**